MOM EGG REVIEW

2017 Vol. 15

Half-Shell Press
New York

Mom Egg Review is an annual collection of poetry, fiction, creative prose, and art by and about mothers and motherhood. *MER* promotes and celebrates the creative force of mother artists and sustains community through publications, performances, workshops, and online at www.momeggreview.com.

Front Cover Image: "Immersed" by Anna Sheppard.

Mom Egg Review is a member of the Community of Literary Magazines and Presses.

This publication has been made possible, in part, by a grants program of the New York State Council on the Arts, a state arts agency, and the Community of Literary Magazines and Presses. *Mom Egg Review* is grateful for this generous support. *Mom Egg Review* is also grateful for the assistance of The Motherhood Foundation, and for the support of individual donors. With thanks to founding editor Alana Ruben Free and founding publishers, Joy Rose & Mamapalooza.

Mom Egg Review can be purchased directly from the press, through online retailers, at select independent bookstores, and through EBSCO. Contact *MER* at info@themomegg.com for info about discounts for quantity purchases and for classroom use.

Mom Egg Review 2017 Vol. 15 ©Half-Shell Press and Marjorie Tesser, 2017.
All rights reserved.

ISBN-13: 978-0991510733 (Half-Shell Press)
ISBN-10: 0991510739

Mom Egg Review
Half-Shell Press
PO Box 9037
Bardonia, NY 10954

info@themomegg.com

www.momeggreview.com
www.facebook.com/themomegg
Twitter: @themomegg
Contact: info@themomegg.com

MOM EGG REVIEW

VOL. 15 - 2017

Editor-in-Chief
Marjorie Tesser

Poetry Editor
Jennifer Jean

Readers for Vol. 15
Jessie Bacho
Patrice Boyer Claeys
Elizabeth Lara
Jennifer Martelli
Ana C.H. Silva
Becky Tipper
Cindy Veach
Nancy Vona
Paulette Warren

EDITORS' NOTES

Marjorie Tesser
Editor-in-Chief

Welcome to MER 15!

Welcome to the fifteenth annual issue of *Mom Egg Review*. It seems a good time to share a bit of our history. *Mom Egg* was originally an offshoot of the Mamapalooza Festival, conceived by Joy Rose of the band Housewives on Prozac as a celebration of mothers who rock. "The Mom Egg," a few photocopied sheets stapled together, contained poems and song lyrics curated by Joy, Jamie Cat Callan, and Alana Ruben Free, who became the publication's first editor. *Mom Egg Review* became an independent literary journal, but we maintain friendly and collaborative relations with Mamapalooza and its non-profit Motherhood Foundation. We've remained true to our roots; while we publish many established writers and artists, there's always room for the new and sometimes discordant voice. To use a music metaphor, I'm proud that *MER* is not solely classical, but also jazz, blues, hip hop, rock, indie, and more than a bit of punk. Carrying out that tradition and providing onward momentum are our stellar *MER* editors, in print and online, and our smart, perceptive contributors and readers.

Fast forward (can we still say that?) to the current issue. The cover image, "Immersed" by Anna Sheppard, part of her Motherhood Stages series, seemed an apt metaphor. With the birth of my first child, I was plunged into a strange realm, one that required new means of connecting with the world and sometimes complicated negotiations to engage in activities I'd taken for granted; one that would absorb the lion's share of my thoughts and attention, not just when the kids were small, but even now.

The current political situation is also new territory, as many of us have been confronted with a world in which many of our values are being upended. I used to wake at 3 AM to worry about my kids; now I worry about my country. It's impossible to forget—at every moment we're confronted with news, social media feeds, and even actual humans with whom we disagree. It requires our attention and our participation.

Art is another form of immersion, making its own space and world in its creation and in its communication. Like the mother on the cover, let's keep our eyes open, gaze steady. Tread water when we have to, stroke when we can. Don't forget to breathe. And let's stop once in a while to recognize beauty as we swim on and out. The work in this issue speaks to our inundation and our transcendence of it, as we navigate our own currents.

Jennifer Jean
Poetry Editor

The Future

This is what's happening now: we're all birthing the future. And it hurts like it's our first. Like no meds and no prep, and no special technique, or breath, or time, or mental room to relax our muscle. This pain is new—was once unimaginable—because you can't know crowning and tearing till crowning and tearing happen. This is the future. And, the future will be born. While we wait, we remember our pregnancy nightmares—like the one where the kid comes out like an alien from Alien (so many moms, of a certain age, have had this one!). Like the one where a faceless nurse puts your faceless baby in your arms for the first time, and you just know the baby hates you. Like the version where the baby loves you, and sparks shoot from her fingertips, and she smells so warm. This is the future. Unknown. Fearsome. Fierce. When I was born my mom couldn't make it out of her apartment in time, I was arriving so fast. There wasn't time to wait for an ambulance, so the other young women in her building came in to help. They didn't know what they were doing. But they were there—and she made it across the threshold, holding the future in her arms as firecrackers cracked overhead. It was the Fourth of July—and the future was born. Which brings to mind a few lines from "Making Peace" by foremother poet Denise Levertov:

> peace, like a poem,
> is not there ahead of itself,
> can't be imagined before it is made,
> can't be known except
> in the words of its making,

In other words, we haven't crossed a necessary threshold. We have more laboring to do.

For me this mother-metaphor has been incredibly helpful. When I meditate on it, my stress decreases, my hope elevates, and I'm kinder to others in turmoil. (Sometimes I'm only incrementally kinder, a little less judge-y—but it's something. I can live more, and give more in joy.) I'm grateful to Marjorie Tesser for bringing me into the *MER* family, and to the excellent poets and readers for this and every issue—because otherwise I may not have woken up to this point. I might not have woken to our world's need for the mother-way. It is the Year of the Red Rooster and it's time to wake up! This future needs our presence, our peace, and—however exhausted we are—our nurturance. The mother-way is the only way that I can see to live with the future. Though, whatever it turns out to be, it will demand sustenance even when we are still hurting, when we are empty, when we are painfully full, and when we are ripped where pleasure should be. Had been. Might be again. We hope.

CONTENTS

I. MOTHERSHIP

Ana C.H. Silva	2	One Floating Child	*Art*
Sarah Ghoshal	3	Blur	*Poetry*
Laurette Folk	4	Suspended In Holy Alluvium	*Poetry*
Mariahadessa Ekere Tallie	5	Sangria IV	*Fiction*
Elizabeth Knapp	6	During The Glucose Tolerance Test	*Poetry*
Joan Leotta	7	Wild Violets	*Prose*
Faith Williams	8	C-Section	*Poetry*
Susan Gerardi Bello	9	The Language Of Surrender	*Poetry*
Elizabeth Garcia	10	What To Expect When You're Expecting	*Poetry*

II. MOTHER EARTH

Atoosa Grey	11	Body Unknown	*Poetry*
Rosaly Roffman	12	The Year Started With The Report Of A Sinkhole	*Poetry*
Eve Packer	13	7/18/16 14:51	*Poetry*
Elaine Mintzer	14	On The Evening News	*Poetry*
Susan Ayres	15	Primaries	*Poetry*
Zara Raab	16	Wasn't I Whole Once?	*Poetry*
Donna Katzin	17	Tommie's Toenails	*Poetry*
Alison Stone	18	For One Day	*Poetry*
Jane Vincent Taylor	18	The Boy	*Poetry*

III. MOTHER MAY I?

Ana C.H. Silva	19	Dent	*Poetry*
Pam Bernard	20	Nest	*Poetry*
Patricia Behrens	21	Learning Mercy	*Poetry*
Juanita Kirton	22	Wednesdays	*Poetry*
Wendy Taylor Carlisle	23	A-1-A	*Poetry*
Autumn Stephens	23	Sink, Or	*Fiction*
Sharon Dolin	24	Cinquains To Pablo	*Poetry*
Dara Herman Zierlein	25	My Old Dancing Shoes	*Art*

IV. MOTHER LOVE

Sherine Elise Gilmour	26	Love In The Time Of Major Depressive Disorder	*Poetry*
Elizabeth Aquino	27	Behemoth In Weeds	*Prose*
Lorraine Currelley	28	A Love Song For Rodney	*Poetry*
Crystal Karlberg	29	Dream In Blue	*Poetry*

Lore Segal	30	Divorce	*Fiction*
Margaret Rozga	31	Play It Again	*Prose*
Ann Fisher-Wirth	32	A Simple Tale	*Poetry*
Heather Haldeman	33	The Goy	*Prose*
Ada Jill Schneider	35	Drifting Together	*Poetry*
Kathleen McCoy	36	Amish Quilt	*Poetry*

V. MOTHER-OF-PEARL

Kate Falvey	37	The Mothers	*Poetry*
Lois Roma-Deeley	38	Mother Explains How Baby Body Gets Made	*Poetry*
Carol Alexander	39	Grocery List	*Poetry*
Julianne Palumbo	40	Cleaning Day	*Poetry*
Jessica Martinez	41	Recipe	*Poetry*
Mary Makofske	42	Reaching The Age At Which My Mother Died	*Poetry*
Carla Schwartz	43	Asparagus	*Poetry*
Nancy Gerber	44	In The House Of Books	*Prose*
Jody Keisner	45	Well Water	*Prose*
Ariane Synovitz	47	Grand-Maman's Pumpkin Pie	*Prose*
Lisa Kagan	48	Release	*Art*

VI. MOTHER NIGHT

Athena Kildegaard	49	How We Prepare	*Poetry*
Cathy McArthur	50	Riding The Train To Visit My Mother In ICU	*Poetry*
Patricia Carragon	51	The Snake Pit Night	*Fiction*
Pamela L. Laskin	52	Sweet Silence	*Poetry*
Linda Tomol Pennisi	53	Mother Weather	*Poetry*
Theta Pavis	54	Wide Black Wale	*Poetry*
Lori Desrosiers	55	The Last Fall	*Poetry*
Jessica Feder-Birnbaum	56	Hospital Dinner	*Poetry*
Patrick Dixon	57	It's Like This	*Poetry*
Guillermo Filice Castro	58	Poema Para La Abuela	*Poetry*
Tsaurah Litzky	59	Sleep in Silk	*Prose*
Gabriella Burman	60	Mourning	*Prose*
Elizabeth Poreba	61	Passed On	*Poetry*
Issa Lewis	62	Tacenda	*Poetry*
Fay Chiang	63	For Xian On Her 27th Birthday	*Poetry*

VII. MOTHER'S DAY

Megan Merchant	64	Working The Night Shift	*Poetry*
Minna Dubin	65	Palm Reading	*Prose*

Catherine Rockwood	67	I Would, Dandelion	*Prose*
Rebecca Hart Olander	69	Malum	*Poetry*
Deborah L. Staunton	70	Shoes	*Prose*
Deena November	71	Mean Mama	*Poetry*
Jennifer Brooke	72	I'm Sticking Velcro Under Your Desk	*Poetry*
Tina Kelley	73	On The Lackawaxen With Kate, 2008	*Poetry*
Sally Bishop Shigley	74	Sleeping Alone	*Prose*
Maggie Butler	75	Tending Fires	*Poetry*
Sarah Lee Cavallaro	76	Bronx Science	*Prose*
Sharon Scholl	78	Driving The Teenager	*Poetry*
Betsy Andrews	79	Simple Human	*Poetry*
Keisha-Gaye Anderson	80	Weh Eva It Maawga, It Bruk	*Fiction*
John Warner Smith	82	Mother Love	*Poetry*
Sonia Greenfield	83	Lord's Prayer	*Poetry*
Sarah Key	84	On The Road To Promises	*Poetry*
Susan Vespoli	85	Bless The Bee	*Poetry*
Maggie Butler	86	Your Name	*Poetry*

VIII. MOTHERLODE

Carol Dorf	87	Instantaneous Change	*Poetry*
Anna Sheppard	87	Stages Of Motherhood	*Art*
Judith Lichtendorf	88	Under The Bed	*Fiction*
Sonia Greenfield	89	Seven	*Poetry*
Judith H. Montgomery	90	Waiting Room	*Poetry*
Laura-Gray Street	91	The Green Of Beech Trees	*Poetry*
Lara Payne	92	A Twist Of Salt	*Poetry*
Elise Gregory	93	The Interior Vacation	*Poetry*
Holly Guran	94	Work-Walk	*Poetry*
Patrice Boyer Claeys	95	Development Arrested	*Poetry*
Gwen North Reiss	96	Oz	*Poetry*
Carol Berg	97	Dry	*Poetry*
Judy Swann	98	Fool	*Poetry*
Lynne Shapiro	99	Sweet Tyra	*Poetry*
Kristin Laurel	100	Survivor's Guilt	*Poetry*
Tara Borin	101	Spring	*Poetry*
Claudia Van Gerven	102	Congenial Meddler	*Poetry*
Anita Cabrera	104	Strategy	*Poetry*
Nina R. Alonso	104	Mushroom Chronicles Phosphorescent	*Poetry*

MOM EGG REVIEW

VOL. 15 - 2017

I. MOTHERSHIP

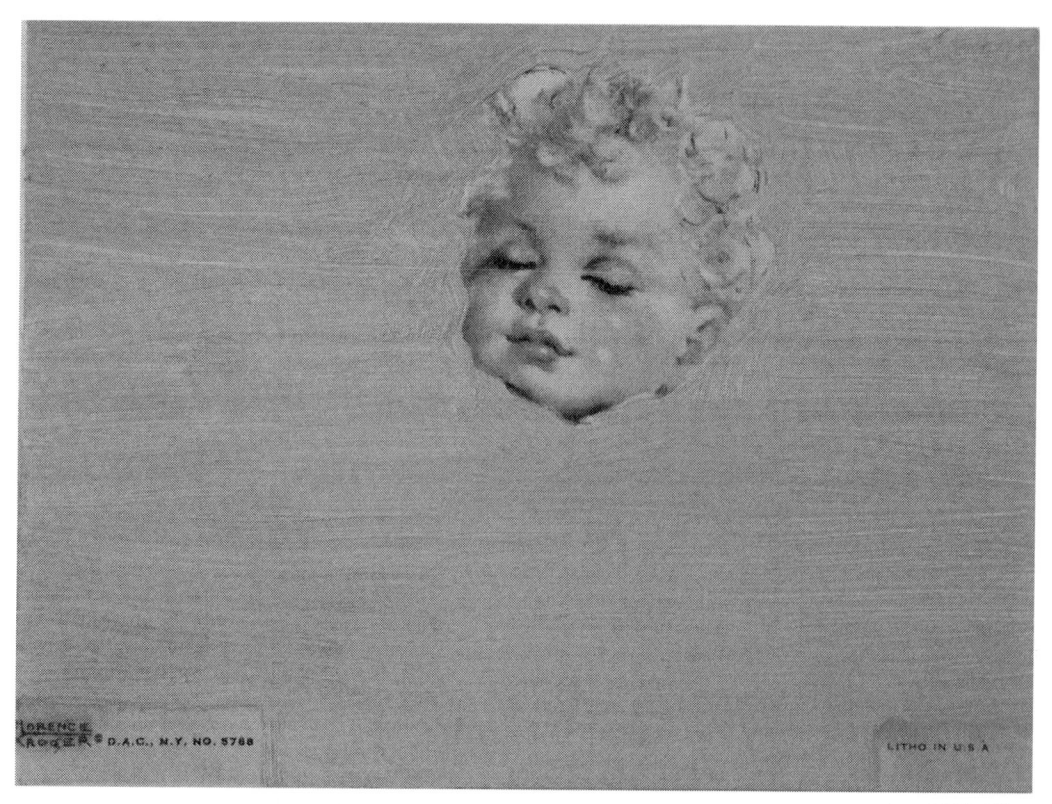

Ana C.H. Silva

Sarah Goshal

Blur

They say you
block it all out:

no sleep, sore
hips, racecar
blowtorch wake
up heartburn,
tests, tests, tests,
feet hurt, slow
walk waddle,
timing, waiting,
talking to you
for hours and the
pain…

                I haven't forgotten.
                You were a pot of acid
                in my side, trying to escape
                with tremendous effort,
                announcing the future
                in seconds.

Laurette Folk

Suspended in Holy Alluvium

We coo, my sister and I.
Spy a sleeper in a vault
of shadows

a pipefish
suspended in holy alluvium.

Oh God, there. Look:
the delicate linking of bone
Now supine, now suckling.

I have lain here myself
with tickets of eggs to be torn.

I have catered to stasis
as a touchstone caters to the blind.

Have learned the tenets
of a hollow woman's creed. But

now I am dazzled by form.

We revel in this code that builds.
We revel in the alphabet of our cells

writ by mystery's hand.

Mariahdessa Ekere Tallie

Sangria IV

The entire time I was pregnant with Coltrane, it felt as though I had no skin. No borders between myself and the world. I felt everything. Everything. Color had scent, scents had temperatures, when it rained my body wept, and my hair would be filled with clouds. I heard so many thoughts. So many dagger thoughts and news of war and more than once Tashem came home to find me huddled in a corner, cowering in a closet. For the first time in a long time: afraid. Conscious of the swirling in my body called emotion. I asked Tashem, *What kind of fools are we to be bringing a child into this chaos? Weren't we once innocent,* I 'd say, *and look at us now.*

And more than once, I'd hear someone's dagger thought and I'd think about the air my son would breathe, how he would choke on it some days, and I wanted him to stop growing. I wanted him gone. Because how could we protect him from the daily deaths? I walked without skin; I ached for my unborn child. He would walk outside of me. How would I protect him?

One night he appeared in my dream. Our son. His eyes wide, brown, wondering; his tiny body the color of a chestnut. He was pointing at something I couldn't see. When I woke up I understood that this child wanted to be here, and I cried for hours in Tashem's arms. Full heavy tears that rocked both our bodies. I cried bricks from the wall of my body because I understood the agony of mothers.

Elizabeth Knapp

During the Glucose Tolerance Test

I have just inhaled a syrupy neon orange drink
which tastes like Fanta soda only flat
and have been told to take a seat and wait
my designated hour before they draw my blood
from veins so blue they glow in the dark
when a young couple walks in with a toddler
and an infant in tow and the baby is wailing
and as he cries my nipples harden on demand
colostrum like egg yolks tingling its way
to the tips of my teats and it's lunch hour
in the waiting room of the lab all the hungry
people like me waiting to be pricked
and did I mention I'm writing this on the back
of my husband's advance directive
which apparently he forgot to give to the hospital
before the prostatectomy earlier this week
and on which is written in his characteristic
illegible scrawl *In the event of persistent*
vegetative state do not resuscitate and withhold
feeding tube good thing he lived good thing
for me and our unborn child who as I write
is somersaulting through the twilit sea
inside me wired no doubt on glucose and life

Joan Leotta

Wild Violets

Walking, not running, unsure how much to push my giant body with first baby on board, my eyes, legs and lungs carefully calculated the remaining yards of pavement. Before I reached my goal I doubled over. Hard to breathe. I tried taking in short quick bursts of air to staunch the muscle pain.

"Not contractions," I mumbled to myself.

Gazing down beside the walkway, as I counted sharp quick intakes of air, I spotted spring's first wild violets pushing out through winter's leftover dead leaves.

Soon, very soon it seemed, my daughter would push out from my old body, bringing her fresh beauty into this dead leaf world.

If I had not stopped to breathe, I would have missed it. Ponderously I finished the walk. After resting a minute at home, I rummaged for camera and notebook—both abandoned since college—and lumbered back to the place where the violets were emerging. I snapped

a photo and crafted a prose poem. The photo won first place in a local contest. I put it up in our daughter's room when she was born. This is the poem.

Faith Williams

C-section

In an enormous room full of light
the magician saws us in two.
Magnificent screams,
this baby lives.
The doctors take him away
in an oxygen mask,
with tubes, in a plastic box.
Birth, or car wreck?
The two of us flat out
in separate rooms
fed with machines.
They tell me about
his light surface breathing
common to premies.
Slowly I swim up
from a hidden dark place.
My feet join me
trailing like seaweed
my fears. We have escaped
whatever lurks in those deep
separations. For the time being.
We skim across
iridescent, light, alive
as summer dragonflies.

Susan Gerardi Bello

The Language of Surrender
> *slowly alone in the center of a circle I have*
> *passed the new person out* —Sharon Olds

I have not passed the new person out slowly,
alone in the center of a circle. No, I did not shake
and sweat, though I did feel the stabbing pain, briefly,
the quick onset of Pitocin. Still it was not enough
to make the boy inch down the entryway.

The boy does not like the contractions, my doctor said
and I was only offering him a centimeter of greeting.
She calmly added, *I need to take this baby out*
and I said, *sure, take him, take him out.*

I did little, sat upright, curved my spine, allowed
the needle to pass between the vertebrae.

In the operating room, arms strapped down at my sides,
the blue sheet raised, I trusted not my body but the woman
who was cutting me open, reaching inside to get the boy.

I heard her say, *Oh, that's why he didn't like the contractions.*
She unwrapped the cord from around his neck,
and then again, *That's why.* His feet too were wrapped.

After he was out and breathing, they brought him to me
on my side of the sheet. I welcomed him with my voice,
my face, his body pressed to my cheek, my arms still tied
down while I was closed, sewn and stapled.

Elizabeth Garcia

What to expect when you're expecting
    to my younger self

You will be spatchcocked
your sternum, your backbone scissored out
you will be parts without sum
two dead legs like sturgeon
and one pulsing muscle
the last secrets of your body
splayed on the table like a butcher's shop
where all the open wounds of your life are for sale
and you will do as you're told
and you will still fight it
your voice weak and pitiful
stop looking, move away
and when they hold it up
you will not recognize this thing
with fists tight against its face
waiting for the next right hook

II. MOTHER EARTH

Atoosa Grey

Body Unknown

Something left
the body not long ago
and yet something

unnamable remains
and houses itself
like a square

in the oval
of the torso.
A category

of loneliness, of labeling
before and after,
a moment

that can never
be paired with
any other.

Rosaly DeMaios Roffman

The Year Started With The Report Of A Sinkhole

The tears now shed for your wife
you did for your cat

At the end held it in your arms
held your wife too

If the dark is staking its claim
I will hold you, allow the purring

Who can tell, who lets the world know
when the sinkhole stakes out its claims

opens by swallowing its closing

Tears get shed for your wife
and your cat

and your planet

Tears

Eve Packer

7.18.16: 2:51 pm

high 93 *ny times:*
'ATTACK ON OFFICERS JOLTS A NATION ON EDGE'
after 9/11
you think thats it, &
after trayvon martin you think
no more, & after sandy hook,
you certainly think things
will change, then tamir rice, freddie gray,
eric garner, orlando, and last week alton
sterling & philando castile...but then of course
5 police officers in dallas, and oh yes
the bastille day truck-kill thru
of 84 in nice, & yesterday a.m.,
3 officers in baton rouge
and what can you say:
stop stop isotopes stop
but it seems it will get worse,
worser and worse, and no
brilliant image or words
for this how did we get here
and how do we get out
monster shape-shifter
universe—you under-
stand the ostrich,
and the gardener, the gardener
sprinkling
the plants, looking,
not at the too blue sky, the
fiery earth, not the growing
green, but the way water
glances off light

Elaine Mintzer

On the Evening News
"And that's the way it is."—Walter Cronkite

Over dinner, Dad waved a chicken leg
above the squad of canned peas on his plate.
He lectured about the need for military might
and accused me of condoning anarchy;
my protesters, *my* hippies, *my* long-haired freaks
tearing the fabric of society.

Mom stood at the kitchen sink, her back to us.
We never glanced at the crooked bow of her apron,
at a widening run that laddered up her calf.
And she added nothing to our argument
as she scrubbed scorch from the Revere Ware.

On the evening news we heard the fracturing
of America: troops and enemy killed,
rioters beaten back with tear gas and billy clubs,
demonstrations and disorder.

At the table, the war.

On the TV, the war.

In our house, a ripping
that would, years later, remain
cemented in our family.

A rift that took decades to heal.
That remains sensitive to the touch.

Susan Ayers

Primaries

The pot of split pea soup,
vase of daylilies,
bits of carrot, celery, spinach, onion.
My mother-in-law finds a buyer
for her old white upright.
$50 and I thought I'd have to pay
someone to haul it off.
But it's a Baldwin.
I send her home with soup and the check.

That afternoon I early-vote
in an unfamiliar part of town,
casting my ballot for constable,
presidential nominee, various other
state and national elections,
and propositions like allowing
public universities to opt
out of campus carry.

On this side of town,
people cheer when Trump yells,
*I will build a great wall on our southern
border and Mexico will pay for it.*
In Kansas five people are shot
on my mother's birthday.
She tells me she's afraid
she's dying of cancer.

The women's shelter where I help
has 66 occupants, including a week-old baby
and mother who's depressed
because her batterer shot himself.
That morning I dispense medicine
and diapers, record the lunch count.
Some women look down at the floor, some
glare at me. One baby repeatedly throws
a metal Hot Wheels car across the floor.

Heat the soup I eat all week,
stare at the pink daylilies

dropping dried curled petals
deep fuchsia like the bits of ham hock,
like a healing wound,
like my mother's lips.

Zara Raab

Wasn't I whole once?

                When, with child, I breached,
tarred and wracked, to scaffold a galley ship,
nine long months, ballasting a cradle-ark,
three seasons, swelling my watery bulk?
I hear the news: now I'm a shattered trope,
a piston pump for steaming suckling's milk.
So I came into being, a squalling wreck,
and lay upon sand where my own Ma breached.

Early on, we hammer out our woe,
smithies at the forge in a blaze of talc,
naming each new thorn, counting every toe,
setting afire the mute who dares to talk,
sprinkling sheep laurel on the stranger's stew—
tit for tat, X-ing out a faux result
till we become the news, these whining, high,
strikes overhead, the enigma of 'Why?'

Donna Katzin

Tommie's Toenails

Paint them fire engine red,
she orders. At ninety-seven,
her ten foot soldiers, each with
its own battle plan, have scattered
far beyond her reach.
But not beyond
her command.

I prop veteran metatarsals,
seasoned soles that have pounded
pavements and picket lines, marched for peace,
rallied for racial justice, moved in tenants at midnight,
stood between black families and armed
white neighbors. They have slowed,
but they aren't stopping.

With hesitation, I apply the polish,
take care to stay within the cuticles,
offer remover. But she rejects restriction,
says put on! —calls her tireless troops
to wear their true colors, unfurl
their undefeated flags—fiery
flamenco, rebel-red.

I wield the tiny brush
like a wand, transform the ten
unregimented warriors of all statures,
shapes and sizes, angles and attitudes
into a rag-tag army of glory
ready to do battle
one more time.

Today I know
that wherever I join
the rank and file, hungry,
homeless, landless, nationless, nameless
who write their destinies with shoeless
songs in the wind, these feet
will march with me.

Alison Stone

For One Day, Let Me Not Worry About Death

and allow my daughter the petunias
with their soft, extravagant purples,
rather than steering her
to dull-hued perennials.
Let me kiss the blind hound's
silver muzzle. Gaze up
at the thin moon without grief.
Then each moment has a chance
to throb with its particulars,
and the river turn back
to a place to wade in,
not a metaphor for time.

Jane Taylor

The Boy

I wanted to marry went to Viet Nam.
Survived.   Drank.   Lived armored.
I became a small town peacenik.
Righteous.   Fringed.   Sloganed.
The child we had was delivered
into the arms of other parents.
Upright.   Educated.   Engineered.
Life twists, swerves, rips, rotates.
In Fallujah, in Aleppo, anywhere
perhaps, I have … have we not
many unacknowledged children.
Shelled.   Bloody.   Orphaned.
My hopeful bumper stickers fade.
Amnesty.   ART.   Teachers.   Vote.
Hopes.   Suggestions.   Tips untaken.
Now I've few firm salvation words.
Only: Hello. Maybe we're related.

III. MOTHER MAY I?

Ana C.H. Silva

Dent

The only thing of mine in that house was the dent.
I threw a green stone egg at my bedroom wall.
The egg made an oval in the sheetrock.
I watched shadows dip into its curve at night.

I threw a green stone egg at my bedroom wall.
I was allowed to have an egg collection.
I watched shadows dip into its curve at night.
Wood, agate, onyx, volcanic glass, even a geode.

I was allowed to have an egg collection.
The beauty that something inside will someday come out.
Wood, agate, onyx, volcanic glass, even a geode.
Some nights I put a pillow on the floor and watched the moon.

The beauty that something inside will someday come out.
I watched shadows dip into its curve at night.
Some nights I put a pillow on the floor and watched the moon.
The only thing of mine in that house was the dent.

Pam Bernard

Nest

> *The nest is a bird's very person; it is its form and its most immediate effort, I shall even say, its suffering.*—Jules Michelet, *L'oiseau*, 1858

Walls and a roof of twigs lashed
with bakery string, set into
a cupped hand of earth—
back-rounded and still warm
as I crawled over the threshold,

sat crosslegged, sky filtering
through the stick-slatted roof,
everything softening to hold me,
safe in my pretend house
in the scrappy field between
us and the neighbors.

One breath, another, and I was
free of my real house—
older sisters swelling around me,
where the mother offered a handful
of raisins to tide me over, where

I woke to wet sheets and shame—
house, seen from where I huddled,
floating impotently, its wide
white clapboards suddenly
brilliant in the afternoon sun.

Though I was wingless, cardigan
buttoned one button off
all the way down the front,
my hands— small knots cold
in my pockets—could open finally,
while everywhere the smell
of raisins, of earth.

Patricia Behrens

Learning Mercy

Cynthia's fingernails bit my forearm
like pink seashells
as we played *Mercy*, cross-legged on the floor.
Practicing being brave, I pressed back
on her arm, staring
at her cold blue eyes.
When she said *Mercy* I was the winner!
Until my mother brought Cynthia back
from the corner where she had gone
to wail with whooping gulps and gasps for air.
Say your sorry, my mother said, bending
over me, cradling Cynthia's arm
with its red half-circles.
Had I done this?
I curled my fingers into fists,
holding in the secret power of the nails
the fizzy pride of victory gone.

Juanita Kirton

Wednesdays

Fry up some cod fish cakes
dip in Bajan hot sauce
stir into boiling water a cup of yellow corn meal
chop okra
salt with a pinch
blend & swirl
stir & fold
lower the heat

Brooklyn Brownstones, 1950's
Grandma is making cou-cou
The air is heavy
perspiration drips into the pot
rendering more brine
She stirs in love, tweaks and nurtures
hums hug the herbs

We eat hot steamy cou-cou on Wednesdays
daddy's mommy sings my name
It drapes above the vapors
I sit on two phone books to reach
Brother tugs at mommy's right nipple
In eight years, two more will extract the last drops
In eight years, Grandma's son takes away my song
The stream dissolves
I am left invisible
and Grandma no longer can stir cou-cou.

Note: cou-cou (pronounce: k'ou-k'ou)

Wendy Taylor Carlisle

A-1-A

Sweat stained the armpit of my Villager shift in that coatless
world where the salt Atlantic fingered the Caribbean within earshot
of the jetty and rain slid along the sun's fat trajectory.

The on and off drizzle curled my hair.

I rode my Schwinn in the fog behind the mosquito-killing truck.
On steamy tropic mornings, Mother's sex talk
folded my ignorance into guilt. I feigned lack of concern.

Later, familiar male faces became strangers, haunted my mirror.

During Spring Break, *Where the Boys Are*, played on a loop in
the Oceanside Tavern for underage revelers pursuing our stunning,
pale beaches. On A1A, sun-clumsy, lusty and distrustful,

I welcomed the tourists.

Autumn Stephens

Sink, Or

Did you know that newborn babies have an innate swim reflex? Still, I refused to give birth in the hot tub.

In the formative years that preceded delivery, the coaches made me put on Levis and a button-down over my Speedo, then take everything off in the deep end. Junior Lifesaving, they called it. Once, a teacher I was having a flirtation with said he wanted to see me swim. Did he actually sit in the bleachers one lunch hour, watching me do my turquoise laps? Without my glasses, I am pretty blind.

Swaddled for a journey I never wanted to make, I couldn't unwrap myself in time. That same winter, crossing the street from pool to high school, an icicle froze in my hair. A person can stop certain things from happening, but I didn't know that then. The life I saved wasn't my own. Not yet.

Sharon Dolin

Cinquains to Pablo
after *Naked Woman With Dripping Hair* (1902)

Am I
blue or white
holding my palms open
to you / no one has taken my
body yet

even
if naked I
stand / legs together right
thigh slightly ahead of the left /
pubic

hair bared
am I coming
toward you or moving back
into the celestial dream
cloud of

night—that
lambent glow off
Barcelona rooftops
where you thought to slumber me / my
long hair

black as
any halo
might be / all this
before you tore open
a woman's face / obliqued her breasts
pulled back

private
folds for your
hairy pleasure / anus
everything to gawk at, own
your gaze

penile
pencils, brushes

thighs displaying their slits
aureoles as new eyes witness
seduce

owl in
one engraving
late / a guitarist's song
horsewoman with wings / no matter
you grasp

baton
for prick / become
paunchier older / dog-
man with woman seducing fawn
I learned

fearless
ness from you: how
to take on your power
be chameleon / my stylus now
writes you

Dara Herman Zierlein

IV. MOTHER LOVE

Sherine Gilmour

Love in the Time of Major Depressive Disorder

For the fifth night in a row, he comes home, eats dinner
by the kitchen sink, bowl held near his chin,
then lays his body down, fully clothed
into our rumpled sheets, asleep by 8 pm,
while the baby in his high chair points
his tomato-coated finger at me and smiles.
I touch my toes to the baby's toes, the baby laughs and smears
corn meal mush in his yellow hair, white beans up his nose.

*

Sitting on the living room couch,
I want to crawl into the baby's room and sleep on the floor,
the warmth, the humidifier, the smell
of the baby infused in everything, his tiny quick breaths.

*

Sunlight fusses its way through the fire escape
until it dies on our living room floor. I'd like to say I watch the sunlight
dim on the floor, but I think the sunlight watches me.
Still on the couch, I sag. I leak.
Part of me is seeping, like a badly defrosting refrigerator, a puddle
of toxic water draining out of me onto the floor.

*

Something happens to me when the lights are off.
Loneliness like a piece of granite
tied to a string and hanging inside my chest.
If I left him,
what would be left for me?
My thighs shiver. I remember nights he would scramble
through the front door to kiss me, wanting to enter me
in the hallway, chipped paint, cracked floor.
I remember the stubble burn on my breasts.

Elizabeth Aquino

Behemoth in Weeds

I walked and walked and walked along the sea, came upon what looked to be a buoy graveyard, a vast space behind chain-linked fence where red and white and black behemoths rested in weeds. I was married for only ten months longer than my oldest child, Sophie, was alive, and when she was diagnosed with infantile spasms at three months, those ten months disappeared, a new marriage and life began, The Husband went to work and I worked on Sophie. *Put the marriage before the children,* the books said. *The best gift you can give your children is a strong and happy marriage. Don't forget to take care of your husband. Put the mask on yourself before your child.* The baby screamed for twenty-two out of twenty-four hours while The Husband rode the elevator to the restaurant in the sky. She lay in the center of the marriage bed, screaming, while I stood in the shower, my forehead pressed to the tile, water mixing with water, but it felt like blood. The books were tossed, the voices stilled, admonition blinded, as slippery as the baby, a mermaid who slipped over the side and into the dark and the deep, my hand on her tail, *swish, flick.* Years went by and the bed was a boat and we rowed and we slept when we could, in the bottom of the boat and the bed was a buoy, a giant buoy, that held the baby, still a baby, a mermaid that slipped over the boat and into the waves, and the baby's brothers. The boat was a buoy, an anchor thrown over into the deep and even so, it drifted, with the waves, it drifted. When I walked and walked and walked along the sea, I came upon a buoy graveyard where behemoths rested in weeds. They were at once buoys—anchored, immovable—and missiles, nuclear warheads, waiting in the weeds, destruction imminent, defused.

Lorraine Currelley

A Love Song for Rodney

in my youth and ignorance
i murdered a young man's heart
now his ghost and thoughts of
our unborn children haunt my nights
what does a girl draped in a woman's body
know about love
i took his truth and love for granted
everything i now pray for
youth made me listen
to just as ignorant teen girlfriends
who envied the love draped in his eyes and heart
in my youth and ignorance
i murdered a young man's heart
now i write poems to honor his memory

Crystal Karlberg

Dream In Blue
    (after "Early Evening, California" by Maurice Braun)

Remember the house we found in the woods,
blue trees, blue roof, everything blue
but the moon? The moonlight made
our tongues loose, I looked less like
someone who hurt you. There was one tree
in particular I sat under and felt free
to tell you things, like *I want to dig a grave*
though we have nothing corporeal to bury,
only wishes. You said there might be
a shovel in the barn, because in dreams
you find the strangest things and the most
useful. The moon was a cup we could
drink from if we were careful. I thought
I wanted to hold the moon
in my hands, but it was your face
I wanted to hold. I wanted to get
what I came for. I was not concerned
with the names of trees that night
only that each branch was about to fade
into the dark sky. The grass was taller
than our fears and it bent
in the wind and I thought
we could bend too if we tried.

Lore Segal

Divorce

Lilly is thinking about the morning, a month or so after the final decree, when she called Henry and said, "Can you remember exactly *why* we got divorced?"

"You always think things can be explained exactly," said Henry.

"Oh, really!" she said. "Is this one of the things that I 'always' think?"

"If you want to argue with me, you'll have to call back after I've had my coffee," said Henry.

"Anything else I 'have' to do?" she said and hung up.

Lilly remembers that it was the day their friends Jane and Johnny were in town. "It's *my* fault,' Lilly had said to them. "Henry and I tried three and half minutes worth of counseling and I told the shrink that I'm a nag. Henry would bring me my coffee in one hand and carry his coffee in the other and I'd nag him to use a tray and he always said he would but he never did.' The shrink said, "Sounds like a good deal for both of you: Henry got to go on doing what he was doing and you could go on nagging."

"How's that again?" asked Johnny.

Jane said, "The two of you are not playing by the rules. You're supposed to blame *each other!*" Jane and Johnny had looked in on Henry in his temporary bachelor digs. "Henry says, it's all *his* fault. Says he knows it annoys the hell out of you that he keeps editing everything you say. Doesn't know why he keeps doing it."

"Yes well," said Lilly. "Came the day when Henry sent his wedding ring to the laundry and I threw mine out the window."

"You what!" said Jane and Johnny.

"Not on purpose. Henry took off his ring when he went to wash up, to prevent it going down the drain. He said he put it in the pocket of his shirt and forgot about it. It must have got sent with the wash. I had lost some weight because I remember my wedding ring felt loose. I was opening the window and knew the moment it went out. Henry and I took the elevator down and walked the sidewalk and looked for it."

Lilly's life has continued in the old apartment, but Henry's job had required his relocating in London. Both had remarried and had grown children. There was no occasion for them to have connected with each other's family so it wasn't until this January that Lilly heard of Henry's death the previous November. It shook her. Lilly had not been aware of thinking much or often about him but his being dead makes a difference. She didn't know that she had relied on Henry's being alive. It troubles Lilly that she has gone about for three months in a world that Henry has not been in.

It's not that Lilly is looking for the wedding ring she threw out of the window some forty years ago. Of course Lilly does not believe that a ring—it was a nice hand-hammered one—would have been lying out there all this time where anyone could have found and walked away with it, but she does not cross the sidewalk toward her front door without letting her eye skim the gutter, the building line where the wall meets the ground, these unevennesses in the surface (evidence of our deteriorating infrastructure) and the grouting that separates the asphalt squares, for the lost glimmer of gold.

Margaret Rozga

Play It Again

If he had been as deeply engaged in conversation with someone else as I pretended to be, I would have sipped a cup of sangria and left the party. But when the blue of his shirt caught my eye and I looked up across the room, he was already looking my way.

    We started talking at the buffet table. I stepped back. So did he. We talked after we finished our egg rolls and chicken tenders. We talked until others began to glance our way. We let the talk lull without pumping it up or pulling away. And when we did part, we did not say good-bye.

    How perfect, how intricate, how complete, how freeing, how giddy, how delicate, how full of flute music, how new. How could anyone have imagined, or actually felt, this bliss before? How full of wonder this universe is.

    Like a somersault, a triple. A cartwheel. Like an early Beatles song, she loves me, yeah, yeah, yeah. Like jumping double dutch without getting caught in the ropes. Like having someone come up out of the crowd to ask for this dance, and, man, can he jitterbug. Like knowing you're going to win the prize and then actually winning. Like sleeping late the next morning and lazing around in silky new pajamas. And somehow the work gets done anyway.

    Though I sweated the question, the answer came with the ease of fall leaves. You're never too old.

Ann Fisher-Wirth

A Simple Tale

So how am I supposed to give a lecture on Flannery O'Connor in an hour and a half when I

have been ordered to report at the police station because some old geezer saw my sweetheart and me lying in the sun half-clothed down a steep trail off the highway in a nearly hidden glade, and called the cops, who impounded our clothes so that I am wearing a bra and shirt and nothing more

don't know what high school this lecture is supposed to happen in because I am in a strange city, don't even know if the high school is in the city or somewhere out of town

and don't have the book, have not read it in years, have no lecture prepared, don't have my laptop to see if the person hosting the lecture has emailed me to tell me what high school I am supposed to be at

know only that Eric Cantor will be in the audience but what Eric Cantor this is, I do not know

wish I could take a rain check because here I am, in some strange person's house, pulling my shirt down around my ass and hoping my pubic hair doesn't show, and my sweetheart is saying *there's nothing to worry about* and I am snapping *oh yes there is* as this strange person's girlfriend gives me the stink eye

and somehow we are supposed to shower, show up at the cop's and get our clothes, figure out where the lecture is, figure out what to say, all this in an hour and a half

but it sure was beautiful, lying with my honey in that little clearing, and the glistening, impenetrable, nearly infinite forest below

Heather Haldeman

The Goy

The morning sun slid across the tan vinyl placemats on the table assigned to Mom.

Bernie adjusted his burgundy cloth bib to cover the front of his shirt. It's discreet, this bib, matching the napkins, like part of the tableware, offering dignity to the elderly diners on this skilled nursing floor at this Jewish Home for the Aging.

"I've met a goy," Bernie announced to the table of four.

Mom, seated to his right, gasped. "You said that to your family? About me?"

"That's what I told 'em," Bernie smiled, "about you."

My eighty-eight year old mother is totally with-it, but can never remember Bernie's name, so she calls him Bugsy. It's not an old age thing. She's never been good at remembering names.

"Why are you here anyway?" asked the woman across from Mom. "This is a *Jewish* Home for the aging, and *you're* not Jewish.

My mother calls this woman Bea Arthur. "Looks just like her and mean as hell," adding: "She was born in Brooklyn before it got good."

"My daughter said it was the best," Mom said. "That's why I'm here."

"It's just not right. You're not Jewish," she replied. "Jews should be with Jews. Christians should be with Christians."

Mom sat silent.

Bernie turned to the woman. "You're a racist."

"Well, I have my opinions."

"Your opinions are racist," Bernie replied.

Mom looked to the fourth member of the table, Rose, who, Mom tells me, is 104 and deaf as a post. Rose smiled, oblivious.

"I want cereal," demanded the woman who looks like Bea.

"You can't have cereal when it's soup time," said Bernie.

"Bitch," Mom said under her breath and picked up her spoon.

"She's always muscling in on my boyfriend," Mom said to me later about "Bea."

"She'll bring up intellectual things which she knows isn't my bag."

"What do you do then?" I asked.

33

"I try to get off the subject."

Mom's confined to a wheelchair now and is going on her fifth month at The Jewish Home for the Aging. It didn't take long to adapt. At the first meal, she met Bernie. In no time, the nurses and caregivers figured out what makes Mom tick.

They provided a vanity table that rolls right up to her wheelchair. Perched on top are Mom's makeup mirror, her leopard cosmetic case, a bottle of perfume, the tabloids, the TV remote, her cell phone, and a laminated list of family phone numbers.

Never exposed to Judaism, other than knowing the lyrics to a 1925 song, "My Yiddishe Momme," Mom has embraced her new life in the Jewish community. "The Jews," she says, "care."

"Except for Bea, they're warm. Warm. Like the Italians."

At the first family meeting with Mom's caregivers, it was revealed that Mom had gained 12 pounds since her arrival last June.

Mom defended herself. "I can't help it. Kosher food is to die for. So, let's move on, shall we?"

"Ok. So, what's your favorite activity?" the social worker asked Mom.

Mom didn't hesitate. "Group therapy."

"Really?" she smiled. "Why?"

"Because everyone's my age – or around there, like between seventy and ninety," Mom replied, adjusting her eyeglasses with blue-painted fingernails.

"The women here…I respect them. They've been through the mill. Good and bad marriages, jobs, raising kids. They're strong. "

Mom paused, then added, "Not a party girl like me. All I did was indulge myself with parties and fun."

My sister, April, and I gave each other a knowing glance.

"I'm fascinated and inspired by these women," Mom said.

"So, Mom," I said, wheeling her back to her room after our meeting, "We've got Christmas to think about."

"Yeah," she replied. "I feel a little guilty about that."

"Why?" April asked.

"Well, I'm not doing a tree this year. You know the saying 'when in Rome' and all that."

I rolled her up to her vanity table. "It's all about the Menorah now," she said, peering into the table mirror. "I've always looked better in candlelight."

Ada Jill Schneider

Drifting Together

Before, after, and always
we reach across
the center cushion
of our couch

to hold hands
like two adorable
YouTube sea otters
linking forepaws.

Like the sea otters,
we anchor one another
and don't want
to let go

should one of us drift
away.

Kathleen McCoy

Amish Quilt

Squinting eyes could mistake it
for a stained glass window, rectangular
pieces like shards of violet because
we die a lot in ticks and tocks.

Red because we've said so much
but never quite enough. Orange
for our range of flagrant bloom.
Blue for what wind does to water.

Purple for the pastiche of hue
and cries we stifle as we stitch
our shards of selves together,
miter corners, place the squares

we're given in the middle. The shock
is how these pieces slanted on the bias
of our lives scatter prismatic brightness
on the blackness at their backs.

V. MOTHER OF PEARL

Kate Falvey

The Mothers

Howling will not do you any good.
There's work to be done, no use
being snooty about it.
Whoever rose from the dust, anyway?
Anyway, it's a lie, if you've heard otherwise.
There are some flecks of old wisdom
winking in your rag. If you think
they are mouths you are mistaken, or
maybe you're onto something. Mouths
of old mothers in the dust cloth. Why
not? when the Virgin (fat chance, that)
weeps toast tears into the scrambled eggs
or frowns unavailingly from a lichenous
daub of brick. The problem is
that you expect them to speak
and direct you when their voices are gagged
with your own desultory need. So
you end up having conversations with yourself.
And you still have to mop the shadows
from the parched, grief-maddened linoleum.

Lois Roma-Deeley

Mother Explains How Baby Body Gets Made

So, the egg is like this elegant queen
only she's teeny-tiny, smaller than a minute.
And it's like she's waiting inside these dark red walls.
No, it is not rust red
like the chicken coop
on Uncle Nick's farm. It's more like
she's waiting in a velvet walled room
humming a little wordless tune—
But she's getting kind of lonely, don't you know,
sitting and waiting for days on end.
No, it is not like a chicken egg sitting in the crate;
she's a royal lady living in a magical place,
wearing a hoop-skirted taffeta gown
opera gloves with pearl buds edging each sleeve.
Her satin slippers are planted, delicately, on the floor.
And when her one and only finally comes
running up the steps, down the hall,
he's kind of breathless, you know?
and then—
though this has been a rather quick and busy courtship—
she tips her diamond tiara *yes* and he
on bended knee,
kisses the hem of that fine silk dress,
blossoming her at last.

Carol Alexander

Grocery List

The Saturday shelves compiled of desires and unexamined regrets,
those bamboo shoots, savory cheese straws, litchi, oily fish—
you shun them, as a child with its specific hungers will.

This shelf is orphan, drinks reconstituted from violent dyes,
candies fluorescent pink and green, strange nourishment,

and you, wheeling down the aisles of assorted trash,
this is when I likely would resist but for a sympathetic hankering.

Wan flowers wrapped in cellophane, balloons of nonspecific anniversaries,
the whole chaotic spectrum of lusts, why not seize them?

The great crocodile grin you throw at me, slithering onto a line.

Everything sticks to us, broken chocolate Easter treats, plastic frames,
a jug of cider abandoned peevishly in a cart,
a pair of running socks already smudged and unraveling.

I can't begin to climb the motherless ravine, down and down,
but you'll need these socks and jerky on the breathtaking descent

and cereal eaten by superheroes winged, invulnerable,
jar of hot sauce identical to those on laminate tables at Eighty-Sixth.
Generously, you offer to let me choose among proper grownup treats.

And only once do you remonstrate, about the thing I select last.
That's white people's water, after all. I shouldn't waste three dollars
on something so intangible, that can't be voiced or jubilated,

without allure or idol, or polyglot appeal, which only flowed some time
through gullies and city drains, or by the lost isles of content.

Julianne Palumbo

Cleaning Day

On Saturdays
Mom would tear rags
from Papa's white Tees.
She'd make a small snip
through the crew neck
then pull in both directions
elbows out
until the shirt gave,
cracked down the center,
and blew dust into the sunbeam light.

We'd wait for rag and bucket
before she sent us off
each in our own direction
to scrub the dirt
that caked our path
to the day's freedom.

Now as I lean over my kitchen table,
fold cloths into brisk piles,
I think of you, my sisters,
in your separate places,
and I feel that pull
in both directions,
and then that crack down my center,
sending bits of my fibers
all the way back home.

Jessica Martinez

Recipe

I boil a pot of *Knödel*,
potato dumplings,
in our brand new kitchen
roughly 6000 kilometers away
from where my grandma
first shared the recipe with me.

The steam fills the room
and I see my reflection
in the polished cabinet doors
so unlike the dark wood
of Oma's kitchen.
My face looks tired
maybe from living in too many countries
or from always wondering
what to do next.

I lost the piece of paper
with the recipe
probably buried in one of the moving boxes
that never got fully unpacked.
Kein Problem I say to myself.

Outside I see my daughter
chasing paper planes
in our yard.
Most do not land where intended,
many take funny turns.
Some don't survive their maiden voyage
but they can always be fixed.

Mary Makofske

Reaching the Age at Which My Mother Died

Now we could be sisters. Twins.
We could have lunch, complain
about our offspring. I am yours—
this makes a complication—
but I am no longer petulant, don't
sulk that you did not bequeath
me beauty. What good was it?
Look at our skin, bloom faded,
losing tone, age spots more permanent
than grievances. Isn't it lovely staring
at the moon, dispassionate, unfettered
by her changes? Now I can feel
your weariness, how work consumes
and feeds a woman as it does a man.

And over wine I can at last admit
it wasn't shame I felt those times
you ordered cocktail after cocktail.
I grieved because your thickened tongue
could not shape the stories I hung on.
Oh, I could beat my silence! Proud
and cold, not good at much of anything
but tests at school and giving pain
to you who could not win me. But
you had. I would not let you see
how much, not even, no, especially
not when your heart began to literally
break. How could you leave me?
But I would not care. I was grown
anyway. A woman, if I counted years.
I have no daughter—did I tell you that?

Carla Schwartz

Asparagus

A few minutes after hanging up, my father calls back to tell me
three new asparagus are coming up.

I had started the patch from seed at my parents' house, years ago.

Now, my father calls me every time a spear pokes through. With each call,
I am reminded of my shortcomings and feel inept—I'm not sure why.

The soil in that corner of their yard is rich. The crop had barely started to yield
when I moved to a land that forbids overwintering.

I tried, but the transplants failed in Florida.

When I moved back north, I tried to transplant again. This time, the original patch
was so dug in, I could not hack off enough root for the plant to take.

Plus, I had woodchucks and voles.

I still plan to dig up some more asparagus plants,
the next time I visit my father.

And here, the generations are:

Water and soil, and seed, not much bigger than coriander, but smooth as a bearing.
Years and years of waiting, watching, and missing the ones that race to flower and reseed.

The key is to catch the plant when it's young,
before it really roots in.

Now, my father gets mature spears. When he finds one just three inches tall,
he gambles on the optimal time to pick. If he waits too long, he says it goes to seed.

What to do with this girl?

I learned to grow raspberries, but not to build fences.
I once battled one groundhog with a shovel, in a world full of groundhogs.

I dreamt my mother helped me dig up some of the plants, and instead of asparagus,
she rose from the ground, full, fleshy, green.

Nancy Gerber

In the House of Books

In the great green room there was a telephone (Good Night, Moon)
    In the light blue chamber of childhood there was a bed and a dresser and a corner desk like a three-cornered hat with a row of books against the wall. Spines like the faces of good friends: black squares atop yellow rectangles on the Nancy Drew mysteries, turquoise with red letters on the Bobbsey twins series.
    My mother lived inside shadows contoured by rages and fits of sobbing. I was afraid but I wanted something: love, which she was unable to offer. She could not give what she'd never felt.
    Books were our connection. A daughter of the Depression, she grew up poor and envious of the wealthy who lived in grand Tudor houses on the Main Line. Her refuge was the library. A place you could go if you had no money. A place you could go if you were ashamed your mother was a seamstress with a thick Yiddish accent – you know, one of those Jews from somewhere in Eastern Europe, god only knows what diseases they carried with them.
    The library was quiet and there was a kindly middle-aged woman with horn-rimmed glasses who helped my shy mother find the books she needed: Andersen's fairy tales, *Anne of Green Gables*, *Daddy Long Legs*. So I imagine.
    My mother took me often to Westwood Public Library with its brick façade, peaked roof and rose window like a church. It was gratifying to accompany her to the sanctuary where she worshipped. But I was bored. I did not want to fall in love with a book only to be parted from it. Books were not just about stories. In my hands I'd admire the heft, caress the cream-colored paper, study the series of mystical markings in ink. My mother saw I was not interested in the concept of borrowing and exchange; I was interested in acquisition. She gave me money to buy books, which was infinitely more satisfying.

There is no Frigate like a Book (Emily Dickinson)
    You can swim in a book but you won't drown. Words fill your lungs until you've inhaled the very last one. Then your lungs will empty and air will rush in.
    You can plunge head first into a book but you won't hit rock bottom. The words will carry you, keep you afloat.

Reader, I Married Him (Jane Eyre)
    Once at a party a drunken man asked me to name my favorite book. I was angry. *I've read hundreds of books!* I wanted to shout. *Who's your favorite child?* (He had three.) But in a quieter moment I thought, if I had to, I could choose one book: *Jane Eyre*. Bronte's novel comforted me in the loneliness of my adolescence. Like Jane, like all unhappy adolescents, I was orphaned, alone. Jane was a rebel who stood up for her friend, who defined her own path in spite of gender and poverty. For her courage and passion she was rewarded with love, which was what I wanted. After the fire destroys Thornfield, Mr. Rochester does not have the power

to manipulate Jane. Their relationship is grounded in parity and mutual respect. I wanted that kind of relationship, too.

House of Books

This is a house of books. I have about 2,000, modest compared to Fran Lebowitz's collection, which numbers 10,000.

We moved last year and my books sat in boxes for many months. I read, somewhere, if you haven't unpacked a box for six months, you don't really need or want what's inside. I was beginning to worry that was true for me, since week after week I kept postponing. Then finally the books crawled out of their boxes and found homes on the shelves and I realized how much I had missed them. When I pass by I caress their spines and whisper as though they are sleeping infants, " I'm so glad, I'm so glad you're here."

My Mother is a Book

In the tiny plaza in front of the Piermont Library there's a brick I purchased to honor my mother's memory. I had it engraved, "Beloved Mother. Lifelong Patron of Libraries."

Jody Keisner

Well Water

"Your mother thinks my water smells like rotten eggs," Grandma says, looking over her newspaper at your untouched cup. She sips her coffee. "That's why she won't drink it."

Surprise heats up your face.

You don't need to bring the cup to your nose to know how the water smells, like a musty cellar filled with home-canned food, or how you break through the oily skin on the surface of the water with the tip of your tongue. It's just a cup of well water that Grandma has set in front of you. It isn't poisoned or cursed. Toads won't fall from your mouth as they did for the widower's daughter drawing water from a well in a fairy tale Grandma once told you.

You've drunk this water plenty, just as you've sat at this table plenty, reading teen novels while Grandma reads the newspaper retrieved during her morning walk to the mailbox, her flip-flops thwacking in the gravel. You've showered in the water, too, though rarely, since most mornings you dive into the lake near your grandparents' one-bedroom house still wearing (at Grandma's suggestion) the swimsuit you've fallen asleep in on her "davenport" the night before. Over for a swim one afternoon, your friend wrinkled her nose at the water, asked for a can of *Shasta*. Your same friend bit earnestly into Grandma's cheek meat, the slip of meat from a pig's cheek. She didn't seem to mind the well water gravy. For years, you've stood on the

45

stepstool at Grandma's sink, washing dishes in a plastic tub, while Grandma sat nearby—the two of you chatting about the crawdads you caught by the rocky embankment and her belief in reincarnation ("What would it be like to come back as a crawdad?")—your fingertips turning to mush.

When Grandma once lifted the heavy lid covering the well—built next to the sandpit where men in cutoff jeans threw horseshoes through the air—reaching down past the cobwebs, plastic and metal pipes, you peered inside. You expected it to look differently, a magical cavern from which The Water of Life or three golden heads could be drawn. ("Ringer!" the men yelled as a horseshoe clanked against a steel post.) But it wasn't magical, just a hole in the ground.

You've begun to notice other things, things that always were but never mattered before. Like how Grandma wears her swimsuit all summer long, sometimes adding a pair of scissored-off pants, but never shaves any of her hair, armpit or otherwise, the blackhead on the side of her nose the size of a dog tick that never goes away, and the yellow ceiling and walls on account of her chain-smoking. Then there's the plumbing: the well, of course, the septic tank like a bloated slug buried inches from the snap peas in her garden and the sign above the toilet—*If it's Yellow, Let it Mellow. If it's Brown, Flush it Down.* It never bothered you before, and it's not accurate to say that it *bothers* you now, but you notice, you pay attention.

Other people are paying attention, too. In a handful of years, powerful, wealthy folks will vote for Omaha city water, city sewer, and paved roads. Dozens of retirees will have to sell their homes on Hanson Lake, your grandparents moving to a trailer, where you'll visit Grandma only a few times even though she'll send letters to you, her "kindred spirit," and homemade Melba toast to the college dorm room that she'll never see, you taking one bite of smoke and cellar before throwing it all away. You'll visit Grandma last at the hospital where she'll starve from something the doctors can't diagnose but will eventually call a gastrointestinal infection. She'll die at seventy-two in a hospital bed—with you bedside and bawling—your grandma who, at sixty, taught you to water ski when you were eight (you strained to keep the wooden skis from crossing in a giant X in front of you), her treading water, holding onto the back of your life-jacket to steady you.

"Is that the reason you don't come around like you used to? My well water?" Grandma asks. Mischief lights up her eyes. And something new. Disappointment?

Your life is something new, too. Something you don't understand yet. But you understand what life used to be. Life was once swims and well water gravy and days spent lazing in the olive lake, sunlight revealing the longnose gar swimming inches from your bare feet. You and Grandma laying on separate inner tubes, connected to each other with a toe-hold or a finger, neither of you wanting to drift out of arm's reach.

Ariane Synovitz

Grand-Maman's Pumpkin Pie

In the South of France, summer seemed eternal. Fall eased itself across the countryside, the light turning a deeper gold. In the shaded kitchen, sunrays seeped through the cracks of the shutters like pixy dust. My grandmother served warm pumpkin pie and cold drinks. I remember reaching up with one hand, holding onto her skirt with the other, as did my cousins. Her seven grandchildren: mud on our feet from playing with the garden hose, twigs in our hair from climbing trees. Forty years later, the seconds inexorably tick away in my city apartment.

Pumpkin pie is said to be an American dish, but my French grandmother had her own version. I doubt she found it in a cookbook. Did she learn it from her own grandmother? Did she create it to use the pumpkins that grew almost wild in her vegetable patch? I once asked her for the recipe.

'Take some flour, add some sugar…'

'How much?'

'*Eh bien*, just dump some flour into a bowl, you know, a good amount, and about this much sugar,' she cupped her wrinkled, calloused hands together, 'then a few eggs…'

'Wait a minute! At least, you must know how many eggs!'

'Yes, three eggs. Or two, if they're big. Actually… sometimes, I use four…'

For Grand-Maman, there was no such thing as an exact recipe. So I use an American cookbook when I make pumpkin pie. But I know what my grandmother's secret ingredient was: orange blossom water. She kept a bottle of it in the pantry, behind that somewhat mysterious grey door next to the stove. A most unusual bottle. Opaque, dark blue glass, with a golden metal cap and an old-fashioned brown label: "*Eau de fleur d'oranger*" in cursive letters.

I made a pumpkin pie this morning. One cup of evaporated milk, two tablespoons of flour, half a cup of sugar, two cups of cooked pumpkin, three beaten eggs. Following my American cookbook, I almost forgot. A dash of orange blossom water. I added a few teaspoons to the batter and poured one to taste.

Then, yes, of course, like Marcel Proust experienced with a madeleine, memories rushed into my mind. This is the drink my grandmother made for us: water with a little sugar and orange blossom water mixed in. I can still hear the clink-clink of the metal spoon against the glass as she stirred. She served it in thick dark blue glasses that, by coincidence, matched the bottle of orange blossom water.

Such glasses were used in French villages to hold votive candles during the processions for the Virgin Mary, on August 15th. My grandmother was too free-spirited for organized religion. Instead, she practiced her habit of creating new uses for objects in the house, to the dismay of my grandfather, who hated seeing the fine china teapot brimming with wild flowers. She probably thought the thick, stout glasses were perfect for our clumsy little hand.

I have inherited these glasses. They sit on a shelf in my apartment, collecting dust. I decide to clean them. Tonight, for dessert, I serve my family slices of pumpkin pie with drinks of orange blossom water. Unaware, they say: 'Mmh, that's delicious' and 'These blue glasses look pretty cool'.

But I know: for just one moment, I have made time loop on itself and stop.

Lisa Kagan

VI. MOTHER NIGHT

Athena Kildegaard

How We Prepare

Coots and ducks bunch on the lake.
From my car, they look like a mirage
winkling the surface. Across the road,
blades pull corn into a harvester's machinery.

This is too much industry for late fall.
The birds roil and shift. The blades scissor.
I don't know where to look.
Someone stands in fallen leaves

beside her car. She aims a camera
across the birds toward three fishing boats,
clouds tumbling around poles and lines,
maples on fire beyond them. Nothing

in her photograph will suggest
rows of corn toppling to blades,
coots ready for the south, people passing
on the county road between lake and field.

Cathy McArthur

Riding The Train to Visit My Mother in ICU

Someone is looking over my shoulder
reading these words: *Help us.*

We prayed these words
in the hospital and at church;

I took a line, a phrase from somewhere else,
a loose-leaf binder.

My whole life
I was driven to this place

by a conductor I could not see.
Watch the closing doors, someone said,

pointing to a way out.   It's morning,
I move towards my mother again,

fear in the carry bags I handle and shift
on the floor in front of me.

Patricia Carragon

The Snake Pit Night

Mom, being Mom, preferred her TV shows to my conversation. She had no interest in how my day went. As I placed last night's pasta in the microwave, Mom cried out for help. Her bottle cap went MIA. She panicked after dropping her water bottle. After my brother reporting how lucid she was, I couldn't understand why Mom was acting the way she did.

The pasta was ready. Mom needed assistance. I had to help her from the chair to the walker. Her body contracted and resisted aid. She then took control of the walker and proceeded to the dining room. As I placed the bowl on the table, I heard a crash. The TV fell as Mom kept rolling. She was unaware that her earphones, which had been placed in her walker's basket, were still attached to the TV. I scolded her. Luckily, the TV didn't break.

At the table, the tension mounted. Mom argued that I didn't know how to help her. She sat down, but couldn't find her calcium tablet. I jabbed her fork on it, repeating, "Mom, here's the calcium tablet. It's pink!" She took it before knocking over her glass of water. She ate the pasta, using a spoon, not a fork, dropping noodles in her lap.

Mom wanted to go to bed. Once taken to her bedroom, she refused to have her blood pressure monitored. Out of ritual, Mom would remove her sneakers in the living room and put on her slippers. She always kept her slippers under her chair. But that night, there were no rituals. I removed her sneakers and ran back for the slippers. Mom insisted that her sneakers were still on. I said that she was wrong. Mom insisted otherwise. When I lifted her legs to the bed, she pushed me away. Over and over, she resisted and won. I managed to take her blood pressure. I think it was normal. She cried out for my brother. It was after 11:00 p.m. when I dialed his number. My brother didn't take her outbursts seriously, until I explained what was going on. He agreed to come over and check Mom out. After the conversation, Mom shouted, "Where's Bob?" non-stop, in between the "whoas" and "whoos."

An hour and a half later, my brother and sister-in-law arrived. My sister-in-law was an asset in calming Mom down. Soon, Mom was snoring peacefully. I was to contact the internist in the morning.

About twenty minutes after their departure, Mom woke up shrieking. She wanted to pee. Her body contracted, making it impossible for me to carry her over to the commode. I lost this battle. I slid her skeletal body off the bed and onto the Aubusson rug. I dragged her to the doorway, letting her rest on the floor. Mom entered the snake pit, thrashing her arms and legs against the door and walls. I called for my brother and sister-in-law to return. They were in traffic. My sister-in-law advised me to place a pillow under Mom's head. Her thrashing and shouting persisted. I called Mom's internist three times on his emergency number—no response. Approximately thirty minutes later, he called back, instructing me to dial 911 ASAP. I did reach my brother. Both he and my sister-in-law drove back. The 911 operator was rude, but transferred me over to the EMS.

Mom attacked the EMS crew. The injections weren't enough to quash this ninety-year-plus matron. It took two men to strap her to a chair. By 4:00 a.m., her screams ricocheted inside the ambulance en route to New York Hospital in Queens. At the ER, she required heavy sedation. For several days, she had to wear medical boxing gloves to prevent injury to herself.

Weeks passed. Mom left the hospital before the new year. She didn't die, as one doctor had predicted. She didn't have meningitis, a stroke, or any infection in the brain. She was a survivor, a resident at a nursing home/rehabilitation center nearby. She survived the snake pit night. However, she may never be able to walk or go to the toilet on her own. She is my mother—or is she? Did a stranger break in that night and steal her body and mind? Or was this stranger living inside her? This stranger claims that she knows me, my family, etc., but she can't finish her sentences. Her vocabulary is often confused and misused. Events from the past get mashed with the present. She doesn't care about her TV shows, nor does she desire to wear make-up and jewelry. This stranger is cunning, claiming that my Mom wants to go home, knowing that she can't. Is this stranger called "old age," the invisible parasite that took control of Mom's body and mind? Is this stranger planning to do the same to us?

Pamela Laskin

Sweet Silence
  To my schizophrenic Mother

Her screams
were so loud
they made
cracks in the sidewalk shudder
grow larger;

I turned
in another direction
my bones a bridge
that broken bodies walked
to get healed,

with every small step
sweet silence.

Linda Tomol Pennisi

Mother Weather

The day she became a crow
called for an 89% chance of rain.

The day she became a crow
lightning scratched the dark
wool we watched through.

The day she became a crow
thunder rattled the open-mouthed
crowd of angels inside the glass.

The day she became a crow
she disavowed her family
of eight gray cats.

The day she became a crow
the cabinet of sky cracked open
and her brain flew through.

Theta Pavis

Wide Black Wale

We are moving down the corridor in slow motion
the fragile bones on your back sticking out like
the beaks of some odd bird, my sweet albatross.
My god I'd give anything to see you morph phoenix.

My legs move softly over the carpet
the wide black wale of my corduroy pants
rubbing together softly in an almost musical way.

I push your rolling IV stand with one hand
and let you lean on me with the other.
Down to the big window with the great industrial view.

January is ending and it's the year of the horse
for both of us, born under that sign of happy
freedom, now, tethered as we are.

The bit in my mouth, uncomfortable.
Painful to ask for help.

Lori Desrosiers

The Last Fall

After cleaning the blood from the kitchen
floor after my stepfather fell and broke 2 ribs
red seems to be everywhere.
Paper towel it up, she insists
Or you'll have to clean the mop.

My hands shake,
uncomfortable
too close to the source.

I make myself hibiscus tea
briefly forgetting the color
pour it down the sink.

We eat in the kitchen
I wonder where it splattered,
were these mats on the table?

I empty the garbage; there are
bloody gauze pads in the recycling.
I bag it all and put it out.

The room where I sleep has red wallpaper
a painting with red flecks
and a red and orange batik of a fish.

I am here to save her from worry.
When she naps, I nap.
At least I do not dream in red.

Asleep in her recliner
her mouth turns down at the sides.
Does my face do that?
Her husband has fallen
15 times this year alone
my mother twice.

If the next fall is his last
she will be too fragile
to save.

Jessica Feder-Birnbaum

Hospital Dinner

Night time January snow fall
Burke & McGowen Hardware
Glows neon through Room 722 north
Pneumonia and pulmonary fibrosis force
The attorney an eighty-five-year-old
Speeding bulldozer to slow down
He holds court in navy pajamas
Breathing levels are checked every ten minutes
The oxygen tank proves more essential
Than the smart phone
A urinal by the bed
Side effect of an intravenous diuretic
Silver bangles jingle
As the retired teacher
The attorney's wife of sixty-five years
Opens an insulated container
There are
Two disposable Costco plates
Two sets of cutlery
Two acrylic wine glasses
Two take out containers
That contain homemade sole meunière
Sautéed to golden brown perfection
Garnished with chopped parsley and lemon
Steamed asparagus on the side
A chilled Beaujolais
The tray with the Salisbury steak
And green Jell-O stay untouched
No hospital dinner for the attorney
The teacher finds a paper plate
Plastic utensils from lunch
The fourth-born shakes her head
The teacher insists
That dinner be for three
Food is love
The fourth-born tears paper towels
In lieu of napkins
And watches
The attorney and the teacher
Raise their glasses
To golden years

Patrick Dixon

It's Like This

    I
have come a long way
to point something out:
   I left my mother
at Memorial Hospital in Logansport, Indiana
65 years ago
        (and change).
It was her fourth separation;
   it was my first.

I spent the next 24 years
stumbling through cornfields and back alleys,
smoking Marlboros and weed, pumping gas,
cooking fries in lard-coated burger joints
        part-time.

I ran aground in Alaska on a gravel beach,
tossed salmon into blood-spattered fish holds
   summer after scaled summer.
One sunny day, thinking I was only a spectator,
   I almost went fishing during a strike.
Years later,
when I shut down the boat on a calm night,
I was surrounded by beluga whales
swimming between reflected stars
        on a black ocean.

My mother died 39 years ago
and I have lived thirteen years longer
   with her dead
than I lived while she was alive.

   "It's like this," she once said.

Guillermo Filice Castro

Poema para la Abuela

The day I took your lipstick
you were cooling apples in the sink. And I,
still feverish from climbing trees,
flew through rooms, your dress as a cape.
My power was visibility. I demanded it.
What's a femur? I asked, OUT-OF-BREATH; and you, so thin,
pointed at your thighbone. *Have you seen God's face yet?*
the older boys at school had asked, snickering. So I repeated that, too.
You couldn't explain. But somehow god had
your face, your mouth. Picture god with a strip
of wax, brown and punitive,
congealing above her upper lip. I liked that smell, abuela. The smell
of the country of you. A land
revised and revisited
by the vision of the gun your husband
turned to his head. At my request you drew kidneys,
two circles pierced by a straight line
outlined on your lap. Baffling but fact, right?
You called my toes *sapitos*, little toads;
batrachians hopping into the unfed bed. Not to forget
the tint in your hair, the shirt
that blew off the neighbor's roof.
How it briefly spread its sleeves
against the sky
as if to halt the burglar wind.

Tsaurah Litzky

Sleep in Silk

When the undertaker asked what material I wanted for my mother's shroud, he gave me choices: unbleached muslin, cotton, linen, silk. Right away I thought of the linen dresses she made for us each summer, remembered her telling me how linen stays fresh and cool on hot days. I saw the colors she chose, palest pinks, minty greens, the yellow of buttercups. I felt her hands holding me gentling me, calming my volatile nature, helping me to breathe sweet, breathe deep, "Linen," I told the undertaker.

A few weeks later, going through her fancy dresses, the ones she made for celebrations: weddings, bar mitzvahs, anniversary parties, what we used to call "affairs" before the pill and the sexual revolution gave that the word other connotations. I was struck by all the dresses of the finest silks, silk shantung, chiffons, crepe de chine, the royal silks loved by emperors for centuries. Maybe she would have chosen a silken shroud, maybe she would have chosen to sleep in silk, to dream away eternity in luxury. She was always telling me not to doubt myself, not to second-guess myself and there I was doing it again when nothing could be done.

"What is done is done is done," as my mother always used to say.

One time before she got sick, or maybe she already knew she was getting sick but was not letting on, she called on the phone from Maryland.

"Your father and I are getting older," she said. "We won't be around much longer, you should visit us more often. You'll miss us when we are gone."

"Yes, Ma" I told her, but I changed the subject and didn't visit more. I continued to chase what I thought were my dreams only to discover much too late these "dreams" were poor reflections on a flaking funhouse mirror. Now she has been dead seventeen years, I would never have believed, the longer she is gone, the more I would miss her. I think of her every day, my mother Ruth Naomi, my guardian angel, my alpha ray.

Gabriella Burman

Mourning

The Jewish calendar is largely set by moonlight. Each new day starts upon sunset, and follows through sunrise until three stars emerge the next night. This is why Sabbath candles are lit on Friday nights, and why the lengthy Passover seder always begins late on a spring evening, leading little ones to fall asleep at the table. Darkness is the prerequisite for light.

One's Hebrew date of death, called by its Yiddish word, *yarzheit,* also goes by the moon. Its anniversary is observed gently, its rituals meant to elevate the soul of the departed. We observe two of them yearly, one for my mother-in-law, Naomi, and one for our oldest daughter, Michaela, who died on the Hebrew calendar date of 29 Iyar. As daylight fades on 28 Iyar, Adam and I look at each other in our kitchen, in the house we built together, half an hour from where our daughter now lies. I light a memorial candle. Adam leaves, sometimes on his bike, to go to shul for the evening service, its hour prescribed by the moon, where he will recite *kaddish*, the mourner's prayer.

Women are not beholden to the same time-sensitive tasks, and therefore are not obliged to recite the mourner's prayer. Nevertheless, I could join Adam, or go to observe him receiving the comfort of the rabbi's arm across his shoulder, but I do not. The mourner's prayer exalts God; I sag beneath the calculation each *yarzheit* computes.

The silvery moon illuminates his way home. But we don't live by its light alone. There are actually two dates of death, 29 Iyar, and May 23. The two calendars keep pace but do not align; one date always precedes the other. The reversals set up a rather vexing dilemma for me: Which date of death will hobble me this year? The Gregorian date by which we conduct our daily lives, or the Hebrew one, which guides our religious observances?

The first half May is manageable. It brings our third daughter's birthday on May 11, as well as color to the garden. Maayan gets cakes with iced flowers at home and at school; I've made a solemn vow to not vacate her childhood, nor that of our other daughters, Ayelet and Ilanit. The yard alights with pink rhododendron, magnolia blossoms, and delicate white serviceberry flowers, summer's first pale blush; Adam plays baseball with the girls. Over a cup of coffee on the porch, I anticipate my hydrangeas.

On May 12, however, I wake, besieged: Michaela's *yarzheit* is looming. Will I feel worse on the date that arrives first, whether English or Hebrew, or the one that arrives second? Or is it the days in between that will all be insufferable, a paper chainlink for the bereaved?

I arrive at an answer. There is no one true date of death. Mourning is the perpetual longing for the life that was, not the death that is. My sorrow rises and ebbs on days that have, and have nothing, to do with the moon. As the lights dim at the start of every dance recital in which Ayelet and Maayan perform, I cry, because I know Michaela would enjoy their performance, and I miss her sitting beside me.

This year is seven, which signifies the completion of creation, natural order. Next year, eight will correspond to that which is over and above the typical, out of the natural order of things. And so the integers grow larger, amassing like an army that will one day overwhelm me.

Elizabeth Poreba

Passed On

Another baby, my DNA cunningly packaged, his little cap covering potential crackpot notions, those eyes ready to marvel at sunsets, the mirror.

Another object of my daughter's attention; fewer phone calls for me. For her, stacks of drink boxes, tears, emergency room visits, fears of strangers, something in the closet.

Here on my desk, a friend's amused face peers from her memorial program.

At the service, her hirsute heirs looked sad enough but avid, I could tell, to shed their suits and get back to God-knows-what tinkering with the planet,

leaving their irreplaceable grandmother to sift away quietly.

Issa Lewis

Tacenda
n. Things better left unsaid; matters to be passed over in silence

At the coffee shop, we sit across from one another
and sip careful words. Ice in our cups, sanded edges
of broken mirror that still holds a painful reflection.

A entryway jingle. My husband arrives
with the boys: a four-year-old who races
to the muffin display and a one-month-old
in his car seat, eyes and mouth wide,
drinking in the world.

I introduce her to my infant son,
the one whose existence I discovered
the day after her baby shower.
You're contagious I texted her
with a picture of two blue lines.

That was when conversation was easy,
before there was a room in her apartment
where she would not go, where dust motes
lose their way in streaks of sunlight
before settling on crib railings.

She smiles, caresses the baby's cheek.
My husband whisks the boys away
to a playground and we're left alone again
with grief-stained silences and unnecessary stirring
of beverages.

Fay Chiang

For Xian on Her 27th Birthday

This breast cancer that has haunted us
   since 1994
      when I was first diagnosed—

You in all of your four year old wisdom said
as you looked up at me,
"Mama! I will never give you trouble
or stress you out which could make
the cancer grow!"

Looking into my beloved daughter's open face
I said simply,
"Thank you Xian. Thank you."

And through the years you've kept your promise.

Last month you flew into NYC
to be with me as I underwent
a tenth surgery to remove
a tennis ball sized tumor
on the top of my brain
that had metastasized
from tumors in the lungs.

As I enter the operating room
you tell me with your shining eyes and smile,
"I love you Mama and
I will always be here with you."

My dearest Xian,
How blessèd am I to see you grow up.
How blessèd am I to have you in my life.

How blessèd am I.

VII. MOTHER'S DAY

Megan Merchant

Working the Night Shift

String a white sheet
from the body of trees
in the wild,

set a lantern
behind its screen
and wait

for the flush of
mottled wings
to lisp and net
the light,

note how some
are frayed as
edges of a rug
beaten against
wind,

how the brightest
markings allow
the most brazen
behavior,

a wingspan—that if
crumpled
inside a mouth—
will tart a tongue.

Wait as they collect
like silk eyes
twitching,

paper darts
that shred rain,

and can trace the scent
of a wounded leaf

to know where
to slip their young
safely.

Wait long enough
and they will show
you how to be reborn
into night.

Minna Dubin

Palm Reading

When I was one and a half, I stood at the top of the stairs dangling a sock in the air, glancing up at my parents, down at the sock, up at my parents again, down at the sock. Then, I let it drop, looked up at my parents' wide-open eyes and mouths, and that's when I said my first word, "Uh oh!" There were other indicators that I would have a lifetime of anxiety ahead of me—my being a Jew, a Virgo, an East Coaster, a dedicated list-maker—but as a writer, and as a person who spits to ward off the evil eye ("God forbid! *Ptew Ptew*!") I like to think my life as a worrier, like a deep love line on the palm, was destined from my very first word.

Thankfully, my two-year-old son Oscar didn't get the worry gene. His first words are "car" and "flower." Oscar's car is a hard, gruff "cur," and his flower—a breathy, awed "wowee."

Those are some good, solid first words! Tangible. Practical. Flowers are fragile and breathtaking. And cars, well, cars are thrilling and sexy...and useful too! Call me crazy, but I am positive these words are an omen! Oscar will grow up to appreciate beauty and nature, but with a strong, financially-stable foundation in mechanical engineering. His pleasure line and money line probably connect really early on!

Our daily walks are guided by cars and flowers. Oscar no longer sits in the stroller; he walks next to it, holding onto the side. We jerk our way down the street, both of us trying to guide the empty carriage. I want to go some place nice, like the end of the block, perhaps. Oscar thwarts my plan and pushes us to the closest flower or car. Every car wheel is "cur cur" as he reaches his hand out. He knows I don't like him to touch the tires because, well, they're probably covered in feces and glass and rabies (*Ptew, Ptew*)! "They're dirty," I tell him. He tries so hard not to touch them, but he can't stand it and practically bites his lips with pleasure as his hands caress the black rubber. Bicycles are at least a 5-minute inspection, and he's nearly licking the spokes with joy, all the while grunting, "Cur, cur."

Next, we walk seven whole inches to the hydrangea bushes, bursting with a thousand flowers all together in these pastel purple clouds. Oscar gingerly rests his cheek on one like a pillow, closes his eyes, his lips moving slightly like a prayer.

One morning, in the hazy dark of 5 AM, I scoop my wide-awake boy from his crib. I'm wearing a short nightgown he's never seen before. When I set Oscar down, he takes a moment to look at me. First he notices my legs. Delight spreads across his face as he grabs fistfuls of my knees. Then his eye catches the ruffled edge skimming my thighs. He follows the fabric upward and discovers my nightgown is covered in flowers. Oscar cannot contain himself. He presses his stubby pointer finger right into the center of a red flower and his voice breaks the morning, "Wowee." He points at another and another. "Wowee, wowee." His eyes look up at mine with wonder, like, "How could you be wearing a thousand wowees, mama? And why have you been keeping this from me?"

Over the months, "wowee" has come to mean butterfly and tree and all things from the natural world. And really that seems right: wowee—all things nature; cur—all things vehicle. It reminds me that things have their place, that life is not always so fraught. Maybe this is fate again—giving the worrier a child most interested in things he can touch, the here and now, while I am nervously tiptoeing through the future, imagining the conversations we'll need to have about bullying and Internet safety and remembering to always use a condom (*Ptew, Ptew!*).

Oscar's words gently press on the permanent worry lines between my eyebrows. His "wowee" and "cur" whisper to my "uh oh," bringing me out of my head and back to his wet smile coming dangerously fast at my face. I've never been to a palm reader, but I can see that my worry line intersects with my car and flower lines, then above that, my worry line just...disappears.

Catherine Rockwood

I would, dandelion

Spring in the suburbs and a big dandelion plant with one mature flower on it appeared in our backyard window-well. When I wasn't watching, Owen surveyed the well and reached in (*so close to the broken pane*) to pick the flower. He brought it to me.

"Look! It's for you!"

Lately he wants to give presents: or says, often, that he *would* give presents. On the brink of kindergarten he's grappling with the subjunctive—discrepancies between desire and ability, imagined and real. *Should* has appeared in his vocabulary too. It leafs out like a vine.

"Iris!" he says to his younger sister at dinner. "Mom made that pasta for you! You should eat it!"

Iris and I look at him, dumbfounded. Soon she remembers he has no mandate, and resumes fiddling with her spoon and ignoring her buttered couscous. I'm stunned longer, for different reasons. Is this my own defiant boy? *Should*, I think. *Oh honey.*

And again, *would*. A chunk of stibnite the size of a double sheet-cake sits in its glass case, on the landing between the second and third floors of the Harvard Museum of Natural History. Its plaque reads *Sword of China*. Behind the clear barrier the mineral bristles like a hedge of razors: like backlit black ice-crystals seen through a microscope lens. It glitters, could cut.

"Do you want that?" Owen says, cheek pressed to the case, blue eyes intent. "I would get that for you."

"Thank you," I say, carefully. "I think I like it here."

Dandelions are more accessible than the Sword of China, though still not without risk, especially when this winter's record snowfall has smashed one pane of your basement clerestory all to pieces. However. Once Owen got the flower, Iris wanted to put it in water.

"Sure," I said, thinking, *No use. But no harm, no harm.* My daughter took an opaque yellow sippy-cup from the cup-drawer, filled it at the bathroom sink, and stuck the dandelion in. Satisfied, she left the arrangement on the countertop and wandered away. That night I glanced down once in passing: saw the flower sunken and furled, its narrow bright petals compressed in a green twist of phyllaries. *Go gently.*

But next morning, as I helped Iris wash her hands, I looked again. And the flower had begun to push itself open! I hadn't known a picked dandelion could do that. All my childhood memories are of withered, shut dandelions with floppy stems, scattered on the grass they'd been pulled from. Did we never put them in water? Was I never watching?

Once again I paused, frozen between fear and hope at this evidence of my own ignorance – the irreducible blank in myself that leaves so much room for danger and joy. You become a parent, thinking you've learned enough both to teach and safeguard. And then your children, through their dogged and instinctual curation of language and matter, force the realization that the entire premise according to which you took responsibility for bringing them into the world is shaky, at best. That regardless of what you know or do, they will find their existence both hard and full of possibility; both unavoidably wounding, and flush with startling comforts.

Iris ran off, and I moved the cup and flower to a patch of kitchen sunlight. Rising to warmth, the yellow blossom opened at full; jagged and soft, brilliant and small, in its yellow polymer cistern. It lasted the day, then, at evening, pulled back into itself for the last time.

I would want to notice more sad wonders like it. I would want to carefully see all these living things.

Rebecca Hart Olander

Malum

This morning, my son taught me the Latin word for damage,
the same as apple. So I told him about knowledge, and pain
in childbirth, the way noticing one's own nakedness can be a loss.
Then he shared the sentence: *Buffalo buffalo buffalo Buffalo buffalo.*
Animals from New York bullying other animals from New York.
I showed him tulip bulbs, the scales, the tunic, the roots, which bushes
are the forsythia, and why they matter so much to me, those bunches
of happiness first seen by the house I lived in at seven, blooms always
downed within a week, and how the Dutchman's Pipe vine has yellow
faces at the end of every blossom, flowers shaped like saxophones.
I asked him what it's like to lose a soccer game, if it bothers him,
if he doesn't like to talk about it, because I never know
what to do in those silent car rides home, words stuck in my mouth.
These conversations in between the computer and school and sleep,
in between friends and sports and head-phoned music, I wish
there were more of them. The words a wet swath on a warm day
in May, after a long winter, when from under the snow
piled up in the grocery store lot, still there in spring, and beneath
the blackened crust, a loosening, spilling across parking spaces
and surprising when traced back to the source.

Deborah L. Staunton

Shoes

Sophie is at the end of the aisle in the back of the shoe store, sprawled on the floor, refusing to remove the high heeled shoes I won't buy for her. I stand with my four-year-old at the other end of the aisle, holding the boxes containing the sneakers and sandals we came in for.

The saleswoman looks at me with a knowing smile. "I'll take care of it," she says with a confidence I envy and I watch as she strides confidently toward my daughter while I stand there feeling helpless. When she returns she has the shoes in her hand. I pay for the ones in my own and turn toward the aisle that my daughter is still refusing to leave. It is 5:00 PM and the culmination of a day spent ignoring, cajoling, threatening, reasoning, yelling and probably at some point, begging. In the past four years, I have consulted with numerous specialists: developmental pediatricians, psychologists, teachers and therapists. Sophie's diagnoses are incomplete, the professionals have informed me that they are not quite sure what is going on and they have been unable to provide me with the tools I need to bring order to the chaos. I inhale, breathing deeply and use a calm yet authoritative voice.

"Soph, it's time to go."

"No!"

Pushing back the urge to indulge my weary mind and heavy heart with the anger and frustration I've come to know too well, I begin to catalogue the "helpful advice" and "non-judgmental opinions" that are so easily offered up by the well-intentioned. I make a decision based on nothing more than the knowledge that I haven't used this approach before and the novelty alone may prove successful this time.

"I'm just going to pull my car up to the front," I say to the woman, trying to assure myself as much as her that I am not about to abandon my child. When Sophie sees me heading for the door, she jumps up.

"I'm not going," she says.

"Then I'll have to call the police," the saleswoman responds.

Sophie's face registers this threat and she obediently follows me out of the store as I give the woman a quick thank you with my eyes.

But it's not over yet. In fact, it has just begun. Sophie refuses to get into the car. Instead, she climbs up onto the roof and perches there like a defiant squirrel on a shaky tree limb. Knowing that a confrontational approach will undoubtedly backfire, I buckle my son into his car seat, get behind the wheel and spend the next twenty minutes silently enduring the stares and whispers of the many people passing by…the people who don't know that Sophie has been in therapy since she was four and on meds since she was six, the people who don't know that my own sense of failure is far worse than the blame or disapproval of a stranger, the people who don't know that there is more to this story.

Deena November

Mean Mama

I wish I could say I was the kind of mama who didn't have to say sorry who didn't have to wipe your sweet sticky hands and dirt creased neck who didn't let you have mint chocolate chip ice cream for breakfast, lunch, and dinner who wasn't yelling, "don't fucking run around in the goddamn parking lot" who didn't lose you in every store, calling your name loudly over and over again who made a big deal when you fell backwards on the big girl swing who didn't let you watch Toy Story II three times in a row, who bathed you every night who remembered to put Aquaphor on the rashes under your neck who didn't leave you in the hot car while running into the pharmacy for five minutes in July who didn't hold your tiny body down to cut your sharp fingernails who made you brush your molars who had more energy to chase you in the park who didn't drink a bottle of wine a night while you slept quietly in your overheated bed who greeted you with love and enthusiasm in the morning instead of grumpiness whose solution to most things isn't more television or a snack who wasn't this mean mean mama but I come from a long long line of mean mamas and I am sorry.

Jennifer Brooke

I'm Sticking Velcro Under Your Desk

I'm sticking Velcro under your desk
So you can press your fingers silently up
Against the prickly sharpness
Instead of falling out of your chair and writhing on the floor

Your teacher gave me permission to do this
But doesn't believe it will help that much
Just like that inflatable rubber cushion
They make you sit on never does

You're the only kid in the class with
That stupid goddamned cushion—
Fucking flaccid futile balloon
They taunt you for it, label you buffoon

Trip you on the playground
Scratch the word 'retard' in the bathroom
Next to your name and a stick figure that looks
So not like you that you ask if maybe it isn't

With your IEP and diagnoses
Your extra time and evolving prognosis
You are tested tweaked probed evaluated
(Allowed extra time that's state-mandated)

The last sleepover party we let you attend
You left your sleeping bag behind
Because one of your friends intentionally pissed on it
While you slept within (his parents offered to replace the bag)

But when we hang happy at joints like the hardware store
It's all chill and nobody notices what's wrong with you
Until you try to tug a small pack of tacks
Off the hook and pull the display board down instead

All 5 by 8 perforated feet of it rife with nails and screws
Who abandon ship as the board plummets hard
Bouncing once on your foot before smacking linoleum,
Denting and dismantling itself, and cutting your skin

A very little bit; It will take one pour of hydrogen peroxide,
A Sponge Bob band-aid and a Kit Kat to make you feel OK enough
About the accident to tell your mom simply "we had fun"
Just like we always tell her so she doesn't cry

Tina Kelley

On the Lackawaxen with Kate, 2008

Wading in the river with my seven-year-old daughter,
my usually obstreperous I-WON'T-brush-my-teeth girl,
I see her looking at me adoringly, engaged, winning.
How dear. She likes me for once, this gorgeous day.

Then I realize, no, she is mugging at her reflection
in my sunglasses. I am merely a wall for her to bounce
herself off of, a learning tool, an object she uses
to see herself, adore herself. I say, "You're looking

at you, all lovey-dovey, not at me!" We laugh together.
She replies, "The name Debbie gives me the impression
of a webbed foot stomping on the ground." When her dad
calls on his way to us that night, she told him, "I want

to sing you a kiss." All we can do is write it down. If
we can help her love herself best, we will have done well.

Sally Bishop Shigley

Sleeping Alone

One of my eleven-year-old twin girls looks up at me from her seat on the toilet, *Bullfinch's Mythology* perched on her lap, and watches me brush my teeth. The toilet, she maintains, is a comfortable, quiet seat in a warm room and oh so convenient if she has to go. Teaching her to go in the potty was like reasoning with puppies, so I don't argue. Apropos of nothing she asks "When do you date?" a hum of dread making her high voice a little husky. I tell her I didn't date until I was 16, that the boy-crazy girls with Bieber backpacks in her grade need to read more mythology, that she has plenty of time for boys. I want to say "girls too" in case she wants to, but school starts in 25 minutes and I can't think of a good way to compress that conversation. Save it for later. She looks at me wide-eyed, unguarded by the irony that sets her jaw and rolls her eyes more and more now. I haven't seen this look much since she was 'bout 7, nothing clouding the air between us, her need for reassurance as pure and uncomplicated as hunger or the sudden bloom of blood on a scraped knee, her trust that I can provide it inviolate. I let out a breath I didn't realize that I had been holding. Maybe a little more time before that gaze, as it should, locks me out.

The girls, after years of scrambling into our bed or shrieking in clammy terror from their own, mostly sleep alone now, in separate rooms, one a nest of books and old apple cores, and blankets, and the other available for a photo essay in glossy magazine at any time, mechanical pencils at right angles and stuffed animals organized according to breed. When they do stumble in, fleeing from bad dreams or insomnia, it doesn't work as well as it did. They are bigger now and are given to sleeping sideways in our king-sized bed. They are twitchy, and talkative. They radiate heat in their sleep, rendering my post-menopausal side of the bed a bit swampy. As a result, I often surrender my territory and fold my six foot frame into one of their twin bunk beds, searching the scratchy, acrylic bedspread for a night of undisturbed sleep.

Last night, it was just one of them, stomping her feet bedside at 3 a.m. until I woke up, turned the covers back and found extra pillows to east her allergy-clogged nose. As I pulled up her covers and slouched off to her room, she said "I want to sleep by you" and offered me her hand, still slightly dimpled and warm, the nail a mosaic of turquoise polish, ramen, and dirt. I held her hand until she curled up on her side, a warm childish comma, and sighed herself to sleep, wondering if it would be the last time.

The tween years have the three of us worried. The girls long to distance themselves from their identical DNA: one posed for the school photo with a fuzzy French braid that had been in for four days, sneering at the camera, the other compulsively changes clothes and conditions her hair. One spends all her travel time in the car debating the fine points of *Marvel's Agents of SHIELD,* the other refuses to watch television with us and then binge watches *Merlin* on her own and spoils the plot over dinner. They are the only Asian-American girls in a mostly white school and they need other kids to see them separately. I need to shelter them from careless friends and the pinch of self-consciousness that stiffens their necks, determined with a dogged, primal-feeling stubbornness to show them how to navigate the unlikely shame of being smart girls.

Putting down the fierce weapons of early motherhood feels like sloth, the equivalent of a shopping cart with a toddler in it containing only red licorice, spicy cheese puffs, and root beer instead of hummus and kale chips: groceries as talisman, organic milk a potion against self-hatred and unkindness. When they were very young, the deep fatigue of parenting twins made me profoundly, religiously grateful when they finally went to sleep and I could shut their door and claim an hour for myself. Now, I watch them sleep and know that this is just the first of places they will go where I cannot follow.

Maggie Butler

Tending Fires

I close the metal door with its smoke-streaked glass,
turn the smooth handle down, lock it in place,
then watch experienced flames try to catch
the new log, an oak that wants some courting.
Expanding metal clanks in the darkened room,
joined by the hiss and snap of seasoned wood.

Upstairs, my children sleep like little animals curled
into themselves, oblivious to the depth of their trust
in me, who learned how to find the sweet spot
where my axe would cleave round stubs of wood,
dividing one into four over and over,
until an entire tree was stacked

on the porch, waiting for nights like tonight,
when I discover I am more than a provider,
more than someone who knows how to make
and tend a fire, knows the intricacies
of fine tuning a flue to keep a slow, hot burn.
I am a mother who knows
when it is safe to walk away.

Sarah Lee Cavallaro

Bronx Science

By spring, my ex-husband's David's attorney had gotten him everything he'd originally asked for and more. I had moved four floors below our old apartment to a smaller place. Mathew lived four days a week with his father and two with me. On the seventh day we'd carve him in two and share him.

    I knew the arrangement was hard on Mathew, but I didn't really know how he was dealing with it until I got a call from his guidance counselor telling me that my son had been skipping school. She had already contacted David about it many times, but he had insisted she was mistaken. She then called me. During our phone conversation she asked me to meet with her, so the next day I drove to Bronx Science. Located in a neighborhood that has a mix of subsidized housing projects and lower-to-middle-class apartment buildings and a largely black and Hispanic population, Bronx Science is one of the city's elite public schools.

    When I arrived, my son, waiting in the pea green tiled lobby, waved to me, looking shy and embarrassed. I gently kissed his soft pink cheek and he led me to Ms. Livoit's office.

    Continuing through the long linoleum-tiled hallway down the stairs into the basement, we reached Mrs. Livoit's office. Florescent light cast an unnatural glow on a metal desk piled with papers. A wrinkled, fat, sixty-year-old woman with a beehive and too much eyeliner sat munching on an oversized ham and cheese sandwich. Posters of sixties group Jefferson Airplane adorned the walls. Mrs. Livoit's perfume was more sulphur than floral and when I looked over to my nervously smiling son, he discreetly rolled his bright eyes at me.

    "This is my mom," he announced. I walked to her desk and she didn't move, except to extend her hand, which was adorned with four handmade silver rings.

    "Hello. Nice to meet you," I said. I turned to my son. "Mathew, take the train home after school and I'll see you there." I gave him a kiss. "I love you."

    "Just wait a minute, young man," Mrs. Livoit said.

    "Yes?" He surprised me with a respect in his voice I hadn't heard in a long time.

    "You wait outside until we are finished and then you come in and we will have a group meeting," she said.

    "But I have debate class."

    "I'll send a note to excuse you."

    Without a sound of protest, Mathew meekly sat in a metal chair in the hallway two feet from the doorway, where he'd be able to overhear everything we said.

    In her smoky Marlboro-inflected voice she said: "Ah, here it is." Tugging a manila folder gently out of the stack so the pile didn't fall over, she pulled out a legal-size ledger with my son's cut days marked in red.

    "Your son needs to do his homework. According to his math teacher he does it in his head and doesn't show back-up as to how he solved the problems, so he's failing in math. He's also failing in biology because he doesn't attend the labs."

    "He lied about all this."

"Of course he did. But if you had attended the parent-teacher conference two weeks ago you would have known."

"I never received a notice."

"You ex did."

"I'm sorry."

"Stay on top of that boy. He needs you to guide him, otherwise he'll slip away like so many…Mathew, come in here, please."

"Do you know why kids fail?" she asked.

"No," he said.

"Because they don't apply themselves."

She turned to me. "Mom, he hears me loud and clear. He needs to hear you loud and clear."

"I don't live with her full-time," Mathew revealed, as if he were punishing me for leaving his father and disrupting his life.

"Does that mean she doesn't deserve to be heard and respected?" Mrs. Livoit asked.

"No."

"Why don't you listen to her?"

"Because she is always working."

"Count your blessings young man that you have a mother who cares."

He nodded his head in agreement.

"Sign up on the wall for free tutoring for math."

"Yes, Mrs. Livoit."

"Do we understand each other?"

"Yes." He bolted out.

"Thank you for coming in," she said, her signal that we were done. "You are the only one who can help him. Give accordingly and take accordingly. Peace." She formed a V with two fingers, a gesture I hadn't seen in decades.

I flashed the peace sign back to her and said, "Victory."

"Power to all mothers." She smiled with crooked, yellowish teeth, a beautiful smile. She must have been one hell of a hippie. This ex-hippie knew how to love.

Sharon Scholl

Driving the Teen-Ager

She would prefer a robot,
something with a button,
lever, keypad, anything
that doesn't speak.

To her, I am a junkyard
of misinformation, dead
dreams, insignificant topics
that cannot be salvaged.

She has forgotten the bulk
of school vocabulary, paring
her begrudged responses
down to monosyllables.

Some distant world clothes
her in a space suit
zipped against the foreign,
repellant atmosphere of mine.

As unnoticed as window pane,
I am ghost hands
upon a steering wheel,
a slab of raw utility.

Betsy Andrews

Simple Human

Unshaven this morning at the living room table, grumbling over chemistry notes, gunning
for an A, he looks like his future to me, which is also, always, time-being under capital:
Hard work. They say it's fulfilling. We can only hope, when arms rucking like wings
around the breast of a beautiful man on a gay club dance
floor, time-being can stop—60 rounds per minute, it is stopped—short,
or slower, slower, if all immunities be damned. Dead ends are simply human.

The garbage pail claims trademark over the sad, trochaic truth: SimpleHuman.
Torn condom wrappers shoved down its throat soothe me, though he's only just begun
to head toward the gay club dance floor, beautiful too, lean and loose, on the tall end of short,
and it's far too soon to take a spent plastic packet as insurance and to capitalize
on it for coming years. Time-being wears headphones this morning and dances
out the door with a chicken sandwich in his lunch bag, while the future gnaws claws in the wings.

He wore a beak on his face that made him look like a bird and sound like its fluttering wings,
though it helped him, panting and lung-stuck, to breathe like a simple human.
That was over a decade ago, when his mother (my lover) and I were dancing
around each other's best plans, at odds and shooting for even. How did I, rage cocked like a gun,
think motherhood, this late-come perchance, a safe bet, a capital
idea? In any projections on future investments, I would have come up short.

Still, here I am, constructing sandwiches and swiping at the news, my attention span short
and American, while the candidates summit the airstairs and alight on god-sponsored wings,
having trashed the set on the televised pretense of the immunity of service to capital.
I'm enacting motherhood like the next lump of vote, and finding it fairly simple. Human
appetite for swimming pools and clubhouse rules and gatehouse drawersful of badges and guns
just a zip code or two from my fenced Brooklyn yard, where the bees dance

among the eggplant blossoms and the potted strawberry blooms, dance
among the yellow tomato flowers, dance their starvling dance, cut short
by hit-list neonics, the national zeal for uniform fruit a loaded gun
pointed and pop-pop-popping at the crowds of ravenous beings on wings.
I add an apple to his lunch. As a symbol, it's not simple, but it's human,
gravity's lump falling from Eden all the way down to the dregs of our bottom-barrel capitalism.

He's standing at the toaster now with a pop tart—no, not Pop-Tart in registered, capital
letters, but the organic knockoff I insist that he eats. I hope he gets to dance
with joy for its sprinkles forever, time-being in its lenience leaning forward. It's a simple, human
wish, despite soft school lockdowns and hard school lockdowns, for the opposite of the short
end of the stick, while elsewhere, drones take to their digitized wings,
and there are other mothers' children, and there are even bolder guns.

In the capital, diapered Senators fight like toddlers over guns.
Here, Pride hits its stride, and he's dancing down the avenue in rainbow-colored wings,
a simple human preening in the sun; so young, this son, his time-being here yet so short.

Keisha-Gaye Anderson

Weh Eva It Maawga, It Bruk
(Wherever it is meager, it will break)

I never thought it would be Matthew holding the gun. That spindly boy who wore a brace to straighten his sagging spine in the third grade was no tough guy.

Earlier that day, I was on a mission to get Matthew to come with me to a college party. The Greens were what my mother called "decent people." If Matthew wanted to go, we were set.

Mom was rushing around the apartment, like a chicken within earshot of corn kernels rattling inside a can, gathering the clothes for the church bazaar.

I hauled them over to Matthew's house at the end of the block. At the front door, I could hear Matthew's flute squeaking out the same off-key notes over and over.

"Mat!" I yelled through window. No answer.

A few minutes later, he flung the lace curtains back and glared at me, almost knocking over the tall ceramic Aphrodite, who stood guard in that window. She passed her days next to the milkmaid, crystal elephants, and artificial while lilies.

Matthew brushed back bouncy black curls that shaded his thick eyelashes. He had the unfortunate condition of being awkward—and beautiful—in the way that men who lift cinder blocks in the hot sun would consider to be weak.

"Shhh! You know my dad doesn't like when people act ghetto." I dumped the bag in the foyer and stepped inside. "He's doing his books and he's grumpier than usual."

"So, you going to Malik's party?" I looked at Norman's mini bar in the den and ran my fingers along the multi-colored square carpet panels on the wall behind it. I saw a stack of dirty magazines in the corner and quickly looked away.

"Your mom letting *you* go?"

"Well…maybe if we go together?"

"I don't know if I wanna hang with those people anyway."

"You worried about Andre and them? Please. No one even remembers all that you lost that fight." I lied.

"Did I *say* I was worried?!" Matthew grabbed his flute and threw it into the case and slammed the lid shut. "Don't you have to go now?"

"Wait, wait! I'm leaving, but first, I needed to get something from your mom."

"All right. But don't start babbling about the party, ok?"

I walked past the bedrooms. Pearl loved Margaret Keane. Those big, sad-eyed children in the paintings watched me all the way down the hallway.

Norman sat behind a huge mahogany desk pecked away at an adding machine. I knocked lightly before entering. "Hello?"

"My name is not hello," he said, not looking up from his adding machine. He took a sip from a short glass with dark liquor and nearly dissolved cubes of ice. His mouth was usually working up something—either a piece of meat or a boast.

"Hello, darling." Pearl smiled and walked over. "You bring the things for me?"

"Yes. Mom asked for the dress patterns."

"Okay, come."

Pearl was petite. Her voice was whistle that played a melody born somewhere between Trinidad and Jamaica. She was possessed of and by Norman, just like everything in that house. Everything and everyone in their place.

I followed her to the pantry. All the cans and mason jars were meticulously arranged. I wondered how many cans of corned beef could one family consume.

"Pearl!!" I could hear Norman yell from the other room.

"Just a minute, Norman. I have something on the fire."

I walked behind her toward the kitchen. Matthew was leaning against the China cabinet with his hands in his pockets and his eyes skyward.

Norman barreled in, waiving a piece of paper.

"What the hell is this?" He shoved the crumpled paper in her face.

"Nothing." She opened the fridge and poked around.

"Oh, you playing stupid now? You think I wouldn't see that you sending money to that worthless son of a bitch?"

"Junior is not worthless! He's my brother, and that's that."

"A man is not a man if he can't take care of his own family."

Pearl stirred the bubbling pot and knocked the wooden spoon so rapidly against its side that gravy splattered everywhere.

"So, is only *your* money?"

"You damned right!"

"Norman, yu drunk and yu stupid. Go to sit down somewhere."

"Damned faggot brother of yours! You raising Matthew just di same way—soft. Mi mind tell me di bwoy 'funny' already."

Pearl laughed and shook her head. "Mind you tell on yourself, Norman. You don't want people to know what *you* know 'bout dem tings."

Matthew walked off slowly to his room, as if he'd memorized his part in this particular script. I sat in the Victorian chair in the corner, trying to disappear into the wallpaper.

Then, the scream.

"Ya likkle bitch!" Norman spat, as his broad, open hand connected with his wife's face.

Pearl stumbled out of the kitchen on wobbly legs and out the front door. The blood dripped from the side of her mouth onto the champagne colored carpet. Norman leaned over Pearl with his fist raised and she braced herself against the car, shielding her head from the impending blow.

Matthew walked up behind his father and pushed the pistol into his Norman's side. "Mattie, no!" Pearl jumped up.

"Leave," said Matthew through his teeth. Norman shoved his son hard and the boy stumbled back. "Ya likke ungrateful faggot! I should have paid for the abortion."

"Okay, stop now…stop!" Pearl pleaded.
""You gonna shoot me? Coward."
I never thought Matthew would be holding the gun. And I never thought he would pull the trigger.
Matthew turned the gun to his own abdomen and fired.

John Warner Smith

Mother Love

It's been hell. I never imagined

that trying to be a good mother

would get me put in jail,

as if I were a predator out to hurt my kids,

> whom I live for. That's my world.

> Everything revolves around them.

> Everything I do is for my kids.

But because I didn't want them to commit a crime,

and because I did what I was raised to do,

what my mother did to me,

I'm a bad person.

> And I don't think that's right,

> because I'm not a bad person,

> and I really love my children.

Note: On June 21, 2016, in Baton Rouge, Louisiana, a single, black mother of six children was arrested for whipping her three boys when she caught them burglarizing a neighbor's home. She spoke these words after her arrest.

Sonia Greenfield

Lord's Prayer

dear lord
please grant me a spot
in the sand on a Tunisian beach
with water so blue it makes my eyes ache
and tiny crabs that tickle the length
of my legs
but never pinch
and a novel
in my hands
about a woman
whose regrets match mine
but who finds contentment
on a swatch of beach in Tunisia
where she reads of sadness
much like her own
yet moves on
dear lord
all I ask for
is a dog who will live forever
one who will rescue my only son
from wells
from the waves
of an ocean that cares little
for what it sucks in
or spits out
from the spiteful girlfriend
who breaks his five
prized possessions
because the boy could never
sniff out her cruel streak
dear lord
please let me finally
write the one poem
that will bring peace
to the Middle East
oh lord
I ask these simple things of you
here in an American town
far from a Tunisian beach
my best dog dead almost a year

and my child
only as tangible as hard sun
on unfeeling waves
where the glare
brings tears to my eyes
as I ask for your mercy
amen

Sarah Key

On the Road to Promises

The seaside ride down PCH was hell.
Seizing up from how many pills, you'd wept
the past night through, as nurses let us spoon
in bed. Your father sped us out, his whispered yell
pressed for how many secrets had we kept?
You made him pull over, rein Malibu in
to light a giant birthday cupcake, your hand full
of sweet eighteen, the day you stepped
from alcohol-Adderall to dance on a pin.
Still broken in my pocket, bright-blue candle
I can soften there, my daughter, where you blew in
                              to fuse a new skin.

Susan Vespoli

Bless the Bee

Bless the baby with skin so sensitive
contact can feel like abrasion
and bless the mother who cuts the feet

from sleepers, clips neck-tags from shirts,
and buys only seamless socks.
Bless the teen who hides

Ziploc-bagged drugs in his dresser
found by the mother
next to cardboard bongs

made from toilet-paper tubes, tin foil,
and flat packs of rolling papers
she hauls to the curb and throws away.

Bless the car ride when he tells her nothing
feels better than being stoned
and he will never quit

so she watches his eyes
stay glassy from pot or pills
or powder to blur the world.

Bless the man so afraid of needles;
she knows he will never shoot up.
Today, the man is thinner,

not so often heard from,
wears a stained shirt,
says, *I'm fine, Mom,*

without really looking at her
until a bee buzzes onto her blouse
and he gasps, swats it

with his bare hand, kills
the fuzzy being, says
It almost stung you,
even stunning himself.

Maggie Butler

Your Name

I miss hearing and saying your name the way I miss
blackbirds during winter, when I waken in the early hours
of a tomorrow, floating in the dark hollow of night-time,
my body remembering their song.

I miss it the way I miss my mother's amethyst ring,
its stone cradled in pink and green gold,
one of only two possessions she gave me,
stolen my first month abroad.

Sometimes when I'm alone, I say your name
out loud because I want to feel the familiar shape
in my mouth, to feel the surprise, the grounding
of a 'd' between vowels, never sure what will answer.

Sometimes it's a memory, sometimes an image—
you as a child, or a young woman,
sometimes how I imagine you now.

In college you changed it to a thin variation,
a barely-connected name I did not give you,
and when you returned to the sound
in my mind right now, you never knew
my delicious relief, as though you'd drawn me
back into the folds of your life.

It's not just your name.

There are many things I miss about you and sometimes
I write them down on whatever is close—an envelope, calendar,
margins in a book, and more than once a paper towel,
leave them scattered throughout a house
you've never seen, when I'm looking for something,
something far less important than a daughter.

VIII. MOTHERLODE

Carol Dorf

Instantaneous Change

No one tells a pregnant woman
what labor or the first months
will be like; that our velocity
is not continuous. The body
demands the chemical
compounds of pleasure.
As a child before gender,
I desired flight, space, rockets –
calculated trajectories and their
tangents. Later all my theories
shrunk into a particular moment –
the curve of a fretful infant
in my arms, inevitable
moment of milk's let-down

Anna Sheppard

Judith Lichtendorf

Under the Bed

And they lived happily ever after. The end. And that's the final book. Okay, now it's time, you have your water, your passy, here's Teddy, now it's time to close your eyes and go to sleep.
I don't want Teddy, I want Lucy.
Okay, here is Lucy, now close your eyes, it's lights off time, it's sleep time. I love you, I'll see you in the morning.
Sing Rock-A-Bye.
Okay, one time, and then that's it, lights out.
Two times.
No, one time. Rock a bye baby in the tree top when the wind blows the cradle will rock, when the bough breaks the cradle will fall and down will come baby cradle and all.
You sang it too fast.
Goodnight, here's your kiss, now it's lights out.
No, I'm scared, keep a light on.
Okay, the night light is on, it's time now, love you, see you in the morning. Happy dreams.

****

Momma, Momma, Momma!
What's the matter? Why are you yelling?
There's something in the closet, I'm scared.
There is nothing in the closet. Okay, look, I'm opening the door, I put the closet light on – see, there's nothing there.
I'm still scared.
You're not scared, you just don't want to go to sleep.
Read me another story.
It's sleep time. I want you to be quiet and close your eyes and go to sleep right now. There's nothing in the closet, here's Lucy, go to sleep now.
I want Teddy.
Here's Teddy. Good night, I love you, it's sleep time.
It's too dark.
No it's not. You have the night light on. Sleepy time now.

****

Mommy, Mommy, help!
Stop screaming! What's the matter?
There's something under the bed and it wants to eat me.
There's nothing under the bed.

Yes, there is, I saw it, it wants to eat me.
There is absolutely nothing under the bed.
Yes, there is, there is, there is.
Stop, you're getting hysterical, look, watch me, I'll look under the bed.
Don't, don't, it's going to eat you, don't Mommy…
There's nothing under the bed, nothing…
But there was. And it ate her all up.

Sonia Greenfield

Seven

A flip book of your years gone
is history never to be lived again.
No more children to come after you.
No way back through screen
or glossy print. Everything with you
is first & last & never again. Your first
shoes are my last first shoes. Your

first steps are my last first steps. Aching
pull of colostrum, pink of your infant
gums, you fitting in my arms, all
firsts of lasts. We send your too-small
things off to Goodwill— you at size
three, gone. You in a high-chair,
gone. You in a car-seat, gone. What

is there to do but squint into a future
that crystallizes like a glass city rising
in the distance of a lonely highway?
I'll keep driving towards a you I
have not yet met because too much
yearning makes a salt effigy of me,
so I become the mother of all regrets.

Judith H. Montgomery

Waiting Room
>*To write, one needs only a pen. Of course,
>   by pen I mean enclosure.* —Heather McGowan, *Schooling*

The young woman in the peach tunic—
its pebbled weave soft as baby yarn,

pearl buttons perfect as a line of moons—
rests her tablet of words on the enormous

world that plumps beneath her breasts,
that rises like a Rosa peach before her.

I've been in the body of this body. Know
how it listens to itself, rapt on ripening.

Wholly tuned to the hungry fruit that
presses a tunic open at the hem, not

knowing how a hidden fissure might
wait ahead, how the body will fall—

as mine did—in love with the rosy
body of her child. And release the pen.

Pages I had written, pages I'd expected
to write—washed in milk and blood,

swept up post-delivery. I tuned my ear
to whimper, called away from word.

Will she also shift from pen to play-
pen—overwhelmed by the demanding

grammar of her child's cries? I could
be wrong. Perhaps she writes a letter

to her lover. Perhaps she will not miss
the pen, swapping lines for lullaby. For

her the other pen might be enough.

Laura-Gray Street

The Green of Beech Leaves

Shallow edges around a swimming hole,
a mineral clarity, miracle of transubstantiation.
Something of it depends on the holding on
of an old idea, of holding dear, holding on
for dear life the tattered crumbled leftovers,
the old clothes and shoes stuffed in the back
of the closet. Green glass broken, scattered.
Rolling Rock beer bottles backlit in a window.
Press of sunlight on closed eyelids. Is the push
chemical or vascular? What does it disengage?
Sometimes you're resistant to an idea for decades,
then suddenly the time is right for change. You let
go the old conception freely, releasing it to the air.
What was so stubborn, embedded, clung to
melts, dissolves, detaches. Your hand opens from
that long tight sweaty grip. Your arms rise from
weightlessness. That tingling levitation the feeling
of flying in a dream, the stuff of myths and heroes
unfurls like a flag in the new winds. The breeze
freshens, the sails fill, the boat gathers momentum.
To force the change before this would be violence,
wound. What was below needed time to form.
New skin underneath a scab. Too raw to be
exposed. A fetus still articulating its fine points
in utero. Then the water breaks and the muscles
convulse, pulse in labor, sharp lance point driving
out the new, forcing the way open, compelling
everything to push this new way into being.
The room, the world contracts to that one knife
point moving out from the center like a glacier
dredging a continent, scraping land bare but
setting the stage for rich soil and lush growth.
That piercing light, one searing laser focused,
concentrated. Your eyes closed, straining until
seams burst rip bleed out—anything to widen
the way enough for such green. Through the pain
that is your medium the way embryonic fluid
was your child's medium, you hear *There's
the head.* Sun breaking through beech leaves

in a waterfall. And then the shoulders, left,
right, and the pour through to this present
moment unfurling his fingers on your chest,
pursing his lips and grimacing through
squinted eyes at the clatter and glare.

Lara Payne

A Twist of Salt

Jet streams garland the trees
another plane every 15 minutes
another day I haven't gone anywhere.
Or is it year? Foreign phrases rust
on my lips. That taste of morning air
and *kalimera-good morning*.
My husband loves the Italian phrase,
buon giorno, and uses it all times
even in the evening. I try not to flinch. I have
known less. I want that rush: language to acquire,
not knowing how to ask, 'which way?'
or the simple word for egg. I peeled
them walking to the Acropolis. How does
such a small segment of time stay in you
like this? To be where you have longed,
your whole life, to be. Good,

we all drape our days with good. Bien, buon, buenas,
kali. Good. Be good. Good day. Good to meet
you. Good night. Dream. Days
without anyone saying my name.

What did I understand? The light
as it broke between pale marble and crumbling
plaster. My daughter sights another plane, points
and calls until I look. She would say, 'be here'
if that phrase were in her lexicon.
Today's egg was good. All of it.

Elise Gregory

The interior vacation

can't be taken with small ones.
Times are set for such things: bed,
naps, or best "quiet time."

Before dredging internal lakes,
the child must be watered and set out
or fought into bed.

Moms must wonder if
a brick wall may be more swift—
a long-term vacation.

Though a concussion makes for poor
interiors, chances are your mate
feeds the babes while you sleep
for a month.

I've wondered where all the titles,
and two-cent words have gone.

Say I was given a weekend with hiking
boots and head lamp. Perhaps I could find
my misbegotten learning.

The problem remains: I have no
maps and little training—the trail littered
with roots and misplaced anger.

Maybe rethink the bikini….
Slip in the revolver. Call what my mind game is—
an internal bear hunt.

Holly Guran

Work-Walk

something   will open
part-time for now
keep the feet
work-walk   moving
an extra shift
make sure to
stand up   straight

keep the feet
work-walk   stepping
one before   the other
hurry late   punch in
overtime   call home
kids   put the frozen
legs   the toes

in the microwave
put me   on speaker phone
the problem
it's too expensive
keep the feet
work-walk   prance
be a show dog

hurry   you'll miss
the train's   leaving
get home late
pause   put the feet
up   take the legs
the toes
out   of the microwave

Patrice Boyer Claeys

Development Arrested
    "It so happens I am tired of being a man." —Pablo Neruda

It so happens I am tired of being a woman:
the early morning rising to right my mind,
the trek past the donut shops' cloying
smells that fail to sugar-coat the cold air.
I am tired of walking under unwanted lights,
past hotels piping music into barren
streets where doormen in smug fur hats
give their gloved smiles to aging rockers
who step from taxis, satisfied for the moment
with their leather coats and latest wives.

It so happens I am tired of early spring,
caught off guard when the sap was dumb enough
to flow. Shredded tulip leaves in concrete
tubs, husks of arrested development, tremble
from foolish hope in the lashing wind
off the lake by the beach. Their buds break ground
like hard stones held between clenched teeth.

What did I expect? The tyranny of repetition,
the cilia beating madly, waving in unison, tongue
parting lips, the body straining to break the skin…
only to suck itself back in—frozen—bound
to the 4/4 time of Lutheran hymns, the red brick
steps of the old front porch, the dim corner
where the dolls await their silent whisperer.

Gwen North Reiss

Oz

Like Dorothy you imagine
that someone will give you,
will have the power to
grant, I think was the word,
what you most want,
one thing that was so clear
when you started out
before you met all of these others,
before the dog met all of these others
who also searched for one thing.
You know the list, a heart,
courage, a nervous system etc.,
a way to get back to Point A.
The shoes were key—
the ones worn for a while
by an evil one and now irreversibly
yours because of the violent way you came
into this world, with feet,
fully formed. You were a bit rumpled,
and so serious, staring—
What an entrance! —
while others giggled and cooed
and asked who must you be.
You knew all along, but you had
to tell them in so many words,
reminding them at every turn
when you started walking,
when you reached the city,
and discovered the truth
about the great one.
By then they knew you well
enough to help you explain.
And you knew what they wanted
and knew what you would miss
about each one of them
when you left—or got back
whichever it was.
The day wishes were handed out like prizes
the great and powerful disappeared
in an instant, waving and yelling

about accident and miscalculation,
which tipped you off to the sobering news
that you would have to do the rest yourself.
Not the cyclone this time,
but a letting go—colors reverting
to black and white, the memory
of faces you loved,
a hand on your brow.

Carol Berg

Dry

The moon is a salt rimmed glass of night and my heart is thirsty.
Where are the small sweet tomatoes
      the striped chipmunk hunts?
    Tight red globes of tangy juice,
      tang like the last kiss before good-bye.

The brothless buckwheat noodles at the bottom of my bowl, cold and sticky.

Judy Swann

Fool

I threw rose petals on the ground
and her pink slippers slid on that silky surface,
the Muse, when she came just now.

Her small hooves have worn every fabric,
every skin, every color, my kids
try them on when she slips them off.

Her little goat horns wobbled and she scolded,
"Why am I not connecting? Why so many
dreams and so little in my basket, Fool?"

By 'Fool' she meant 'Innocent Child.'
She said, and I could see her beard,
she said, "Tell me that you love me."

"I am," I said, "not sleeping alone."
She said, "Tell me that you love me."
I said she was always on my mind, I called

As often as I could. She said, "Tell me
that you love me." I said "I've spent twenty years,
two husbands, and all my thrift on those roses."

Lynne Shapiro

Sweet Tyra Suite, Adieu

Are you shaken like a tipsy cocktail when I *smize* and confess
I watched America's Best Top Model? I know, I know, doesn't fit
your image of me, that confection of a TV show - but it was educational,
models modeled modeling, how to pose for a *killa* picture, how to learn
what I thought only came naturally. I've seen women and men transmute
homely and awkward into golden stills (skills?) while some beauties
have no model magic, can't shape themselves into pleasing pretzels,
power cupcakes, or digitally twisted tarts.

I myself suffer from Breugel Syndrome, unable to take pictures with eyes
open. My magic? I synch a blink when the shutter clicks; I've a sixth sense
of snappishness. Surrealists in photo booths, eyes shut, paid homage
to automatic writers, sleepers, and dreamers who believed that eyelids,
like shut doors, permitted a final reveal of some interior planet.
That's what the winning-est top models know. Take our picture!
All of us! With red velvet and seven layer. You, on the cake stand!
Me covered in frosting. The blond with maraschino wig -
give a *booty tooch* to the guy in the fondant kimono.

Kristin Laurel

Survivor's Guilt

i.
Last spring I found a nest of garter snakes under my front doorstep. I killed them all, even the little ones. I yelled at my dog, *you could help me you big chicken.* The neighbors across the street told me they laughed as they watched through their kitchen window. I wasn't embarrassed that they saw me out there screaming in my pajamas pounding the ground with that shovel. But afterwards I worried about my karma. I even dreamed about those baby snakes; I dreamed I killed all the babies and the mama snake was still alive. She hissed at me, and said, *You'll pay for this someday.* I woke up feeling scared. But mostly, I felt guilty.

ii.
When the kids were little we lived in the country and the snakes stayed away from the house, back by the pond. I remember my three kids and my nephew used to catch them and play circus. They would chase them through the grass, poke them with sticks, drop them in buckets and give them zip-line rides on the clothesline; they'd bury them in the sandbox and put them in their swimming pool. Eventually they let them go. None of the snakes ever died, but my sister's children did. My sister tried to kill herself after that, but I don't want to die. Now I live guiltily in a house with grown-up children and two dead nephews. And everyone is scared of snakes.

iii.
This spring I saw three little sneaky snakes sticking their tongues out at me from under my front porch. I bought some smoke bombs; tried to smoke them all with sulfur but now my basement smells like rotten eggs. I tried to drown them with a garden hose, and sprayed myself instead. I spread the area with mothballs but those little suckers are stubborn and they still won't go away. It's not like they're poisonous, but it's painful if they bite. I could get a staphylococcus infection that's antibiotic-resistant; I could lose a limb, become septic or even die. I can't let them take over. I guess we're going to have to sort of co-exist. I'm going to catch them, turn them loose in the marsh and tell those sons of bitches, *If you all want to live, stay the hell out of my yard!*

Tara Borin

Spring

Most days I am a black billow
of clouds that choke
their horizon.

I trudge through the thick,
oblivious to miracles
both large and
small:

sun touching frost's retreat,

last summer's shoes
outgrown,

wood frog heart
reanimated.

A startle of grouse or
a child's hand slipped into mine
causes me to
break.

Buds burst,
the world
greening like a smile.

Claudia Van Gerven

Congenial Meddler

Let's say, evening will open like a lavender orchid—
OK.   Maybe not.

But to say it, anyway, to feel that moist skin, the indefinite
flesh of the sound

a laugh like a silk sleeve fluttering to a samba
of whispers

the vibration as between a mother and child
a subcutaneous knowing

the way a harp string can sing a swarm of notes,
how you can

feel the sounds in your fingerends, even if you've
never played.

There's just that hum between the word and
everywhere you've

never been, that movement of voluptuous memories
you're pretty sure

never happened. But why not go there anyway?
You've been

here before—and after, the light ricocheting
a reversible

diamond, the syllables true as any history
book. Because

it's beautiful, because it's there, that evening
unfolding its curved

petals, the tilted violet gravity of words bending
this time, this space.

Anita Cabrera

Strategy

Empty
boxes
of all
creatures.
Release

varmint, boy, and bug. Unfold the cloth that swaddles Unpin
limbs, unbend arms pressed to breast. Raise window. Take knife.
Slice screen, a hole to wriggle through. Avoid smashed cheeks or
chins, or beaks on glass. Cut cord. Break shell. Unscrew lid. Shake
out contents. Watch wings and legs in concert. Free pheromone and fur.

Open
door.
Kiss
wind.

Nina R. Alonso

Mushroom Chronicles Phosphorescent

the ones in the photos aren't
cooked or chopped or sauteed
in her black iron pan

stove's spattered from whatever fried
last night too tired to notice the mess
whatever she can manage after work

is throw something
on the fire get rawness out
wait until onions turn

that cookbook term 'translucent'
eat by the drowning drumming tv
rolling quasi-obscene rosaries of ads

political smears blistering lies
telling you to order your doctor
to mend pain with whatever they're selling

no these are aesthetic mushrooms
circling through time like half-tutus
at the rotting base of a great tree

vibrating in forests drunk on
sun-filtered silence loftiest
branches exhaling sounds

hypnotic to a dreamer's ear
meditative hum of phosphorescent
fungi singing through the night.

CONTRIBUTORS' NOTES

Carol Alexander's poems have appeared in numerous anthologies and journals, among them *Bluestem, The Canary, Chiron Review, The Common, Mobius, Poetica, Poetry Quarterly, Poetrybay, Split Rock Review,* and *The San Pedro River Review.* Work is forthcoming in *Driftwood Press, The American Journal of Poetry,* and *CHEST.* Alexander's chapbook *Bridal Veil Falls* is published by Flutter Press. Her full-length poetry collection, *Habit Lost,* is forthcoming from Cave Moon Press.

Nina R. Alonso's work appeared in *U. Mass. Review, The New Yorker, Sumac, WomenPoems, Ploughshares, Ibbetson Street, Muddy River Poetry Review, Constant Remembrance, Black Poppy Review, Wilderness House Literary Review,* and others. Her stories were in *Southern Women's Review, Tears and Laughter, Broadkill Review,* and others. Her book *This Body* was published by David Godine Press. She teaches at Fresh Pond Ballet School and meditates with heartfulness.org.

Keisha-Gaye Anderson is a Jamaican-born poet and creative writer living in Brooklyn, NY. She is the author of the poetry collection *Gathering the Waters* (Jamii Publishing). Her writing has been published in *Interviewing the Caribbean, Renaissance Noire, The Killens Review of Arts and Letters, Mosaic Literary Magazine, African Voices Magazine,* and others. A past participant of the VONA Voices and Callaloo Creative Writing workshops, Keisha was named a fellow by the North Country Institute for Writers of Color. Keisha holds an M.F.A. in Creative Writing from The City College, CUNY. Follow her on Twitter @KeishaGaye1.

Betsy Andrews is the author of *The Bottom* (42 Miles Press), which was winner of the 42 Miles Press Prize in Poetry, and *New Jersey* (2007, University of Wisconsin Press), which was the winner of the Brittingham Prize in Poetry. https://betsyandrews.contently.com/

Elizabeth Aquino is a writer living in Los Angeles with her three children, the oldest of whom is a young adult with severe disabilities who has inspired much of her mother's recent work. Published in several literary anthologies, *The Los Angeles Times,* and *Spirituality and Health,* Elizabeth is currently working on a book of creative nonfiction. Honors include a writing residency from Hedgebrook on Whidbey Island and a fellowship to work under Lidia Yuknavitch at Tomales Bay. She also blogs daily at www.elizabethaquino.blogspot.com and lives a life of vast freedom and leisure with her daughter and two teenaged boys.

Susan Ayres teaches at Texas A&M University School of Law in Fort Worth, Texas. She is also pursuing an MFA in writing at Vermont College of Fine Arts. Her poems have appeared in *descant, Kalliope, Texas Review, Borderlands, Barely South Review,* and other journals.

Patricia Behrens lives in Manhattan on the Upper West Side. Her poetry has appeared previously in *Mom Egg Review* and also in *American Arts Quarterly, The Main Street Rag, The Same, Perfume River Review* and elsewhere. She is a lawyer and co-editor of *Courthouses of the Second Circuit: Their Architecture, History, and Stories* (Acanthus Press 2015).

Susan Gerardi Bello is an Editor at U.S. 1 Worksheets, a poetry journal based in Princeton, NJ. Susan also curates a monthly poetry series at the Newtown Library Company in her current hometown of Newtown, Pa. Her poems "Janis Joplin as Postage Stamp" and "The Game" were nominated for a Pushcart Prize.

Carol Berg's poems are forthcoming or in *Sou'wester, The Journal, Spillway, Redactions, Zone 3,* and elsewhere. Her chapbook, *Her Vena Amoris* (Red Bird Chapbooks), is available and her chapbooks, *Ophelia Unraveling* and *The Ornithologist Poems* are available from Dancing Girl Press.

Pam Bernard, a poet, painter, editor, and adjunct professor, received her MFA in Creative Writing from Warren Wilson College, and BA from Harvard University. Her awards include a National Endowment for the Arts Fellowship in Poetry, two Massachusetts Cultural Council Fellowships, the Grolier Prize in Poetry, and a MacDowell Fellowship. She has published three full-length collections of poetry, and a verse novel entitled *Esther,* published by CavanKerry Press. Ms. Bernard lives in Walpole, New Hampshire, and teaches writing at Franklin Pierce University and conducts private workshops. http://www.pambernard.com/

Tara Borin lives and writes in Dawson City, Yukon, Canada. Her poetry has recently appeared in *Petal Journal*, *Yellow Chair Review* and *Uppagus*. More of her work can be found online at http://taraborinwrites.com

Jennifer Brooke has been ridiculously fortunate to study poetry with Billy Collins. She has had poetry and essays published by *TSR-The Southampton Review*, *The East Hampton Star*, *RFD Magazine*, *The Sun*, *Hartskill Review*, *Rubbertop Review*, and *Mom Egg Review*. Brooke's misspent youth was spent in advertising. Brooke and her wife, Beatrice Alda, raised five children together over the past 13 years, and her writing is generally either a casualty or result of their blended family.

Gabriella Burman writes non-fiction from her home in suburban Detroit. A chapbook of essays, *Michaela*, was published by the Michigan Writers' Cooperative Press in 2015. Follow her on twitter @gabriellaburman.

Maggie Butler—daughter, mother, and grandmother—leads creative writing workshops on the coast of Maine and Ireland. Her poetry has appeared in the *Aurorean*, *Crannóg Literary Magazine*, *The Naugatuck River Review*, and an anthology, *Journey to Crone*. A Maine Literary Award recipient and a Best Screenplay award winner (Moondance International Film Festival), Maggie is currently wrestling with a novel.

Anita Cabrera's work has appeared in *The Berkeley Fiction Review*, *The Berkeley Poetry Review*, *Brain, Child Magazine*, *Colere*, *Acentos Review*, and the *Squaw Valley Poetry Review*, and she was recently named winner of The New Guard's Machigonne Fiction Contest. She lives and teaches San Francisco, CA.

Wendy Taylor Carlisle grew up in Ft Lauderdale, Florida and lives now in the Ozarks. She is the author of two books and five chapbooks. See more of her work at www.wendytaylorcarlisle.com.

Patricia Carragon has two forthcoming books: *Cupcake Chronicles* (Poets Wear Prada) and *Innocence* (Finishing Line Press). She hosts the Brooklyn-based Brownstone Poets and is the editor-in-chief of its annual anthology. Patricia is one of the Executive Editors for Home Planet News Online.

Guillermo Filice Castro is a poet and photographer. He's the author of the poetry chapbook *Agua, Fuego* (Finishing Line Press, 2015) and the recipient of an E-S-B fellowship from the Poetry Project. Born and raised in Argentina, Castro lives in New York City. https://www.instagram.com/guillermo_f_castro/

Sarah Lee Cavallaro is the former president/executive producer of award-winning Emerald Films, a TV commercial production company. Her novel *Dogs Have Angels Too* won Best in Women's Fiction from the Indie Reader Discovery Awards. She is a poet published in numerous anthologies. She has produced provocative art installations for the renowned artist Cosimo Cavallaro. www.dogshaveangelstoo.com

Fay Chiang is a poet and visual artist who believes culture is a spiritual and psychological weapon used for the empowerment of people and communities. Working at Project Reach, a youth center for young people at risk in Chinatown and the Lower East Side, she is also a member of Zero Capital, an artists collective; the Orchard Street Advocacy and Wellness Center, which supports people living with HIV/AIDS, cancer and other chronic illnesses. Battling her 8th bout of breast cancer, she is working on her memoir. *Seven Continents Nine Lives* (Bowery Books) is her most recent collection of poetry. And she is the mother of the inimitable Xian.

Patrice Boyer Claeys is enjoying the freedom of the empty nest. She thanks her writing group, Serious Play, for keeping her chiseling away. A reader for *Mom Egg*, she is celebrating her fifth year of publication in that review. Her work has appeared in *Found Poetry Review*, *Blue Heron*, *Avocet*, *ARDOR* and the *NWCC Chapbook*. She was nominated for Best of the Net.

Lorraine Currelley is a poet, writer, storyteller, multidisciplinary artist, activist, and mental health and grief & bereavement counselor. Executive Director, Poets Network & Exchange, Inc. Anthologized and awards recipient. Publications include but are not limited to *Mom Egg Review*, *DoveTales*, Belladonna, Blind Beggar Press, and *Poets/Artists Magazine*. Awards, 2015 NYPL Arts for A Lifetime Grant, SPARC Residency and Out of the Binders Scholar. Poets & Writers 2015 Cross Cultural reading. Spotlighted by the Association of Writers and Writing Programs and Poets & Writers in 2016. http://www.poetsnetworkandexchange.com/

Lori Desrosiers' poetry books are *The Philosopher's Daughter* (Salmon Poetry, 2013), a chapbook, *Inner Sky* (Glass Lyre Press 2015) and *Sometimes I Hear the Clock Speak* (Salmon Poetry, 2016). Her work has been nominated for a Pushcart Prize. She edits Naugatuck River Review, a journal of narrative poetry. http://loridesrosierspoetry.com

Patrick Dixon is a writer and photographer retired from careers in teaching and commercial fishing who lives in Olympia, Washington. He has been published in *Cirque Literary Journal, The Journal of Family Life, Oberon Poetry Journal,* and others. His chapbook *Arc of Visibility* won the 2015 Alabama State Poetry Morris Memorial competition. His work may be seen at www.PatrickDixon.net.

Sharon Dolin is the author of six poetry collections, most recently, *Manual for Living*, published by the University of Pittsburgh Press in 2016. The recipient of a 2016 PEN/Heim Translation Fund grant for her translations from the Catalan, she directs and teaches in Writing About Art in Barcelona each June. http://www.sharondolin.com/barcelona-workshops/

Carol Dorf's chapbook, *Theory Headed Dragon*, is available through Finishing Line Press. Her poetry has been published in *Glint, Slipstream, Spillway, Sin Fronteras, Antiphon, About Place, The Journal of Humanistic Mathematics, Scientific American, Maintenant, OVS, Best of Indie Lit New England,* and elsewhere. She is poetry editor of *Talking Writing* and teaches mathematics in Berkeley, CA. http://momeggreview.com/2017/01/03/theory-headed-dragon-by-carol-dorf/

Minna Dubin is a writer, performer, and educator. She is the founder of #MomLists, a Bay Area literary public art project. Her work has been featured in *MUTHA Magazine, The Forward,* and various literary magazines. When not chasing her toddler in circles around the dining room table, she is eating chocolate in the bathroom while texting.

Kate Falvey's work has been widely published in journals and anthologies, including four previous issues of *Mom Egg Review*. Her first full length collection, *The Language of Little Girls*, was published in 2016 by David Robert Books. She edits the *2 Bridges Review*, published through the New York City College of Technology of the City University of New York, where she teaches, and is an Associate Editor of NYU Langone Medical Center's *Bellevue Literary Review*.

Jessica Feder-Birnbaum is a playwright, author, director and teaching artist. Her monologue, Midlife Choice, is among the selected works in the Reproductive Freedom Festival Anthology, published by Indie Theatre Now. Her articles appear in print and on line.

Ann Fisher-Wirth's fifth book of poems, *Mississippi*, is forthcoming from Wings Press in 2017; this is a poetry/photography collaboration with Maude Schuyler Clay. Ann is coeditor (with Laura-Gray Street) of The Ecopoetry Anthology and author of *Dream Cabinet, Carta Marina,* and other books. A fellow of the Black Earth Institute, recipient of numerous residencies and awards, she teaches at the University of Mississippi.

Laurette Folk's fiction, essays, and poems have been published in *upstreet, Literary Mama, Boston Globe Magazine, Talking Writing, Narrative Northeast, So to Speak* among others. Her novel, A *Portal to Vibrancy*, was published by Big Table; Totem Beasts, her collection of poetry and flash fiction, is forthcoming from Big Table in 2017. Ms. Folk is a graduate of the Vermont College MFA in Writing program and editor of *The Compassion Anthology*. http://www.laurettefolk.com/

Elizabeth Garcia's work has appeared in numerous journals and in two recent anthologies, *Stone, River, Sky: An Anthology of Georgia Poems,* and *Fire in the Pasture: 21st Century Mormon Poets*. She is currently a stay-at-home-mom of two little ones and has her first chapbook, *Stunt Double*, out by Finishing Line Press. Visit elizabethcgarcia.wordpress.com for more information.

Nancy Gerber is an advanced candidate in psychoanalytic training at the Academy of Clinical and Applied Psychoanalysis in Livingston, NJ. Her most recent book, *Fire and Ice: Poetry and Prose* (Arseya, 2014), was nominated for a Gradiva Award in Poetry from the National Association for the Advancement of Psychoanalysis and was named a Notable Book in the 2014 Shelf Unbound Indie Books Competition.

Sarah Ghoshal is a poet, a mom, a professor and a runner. She has published two poetry chapbooks and her work can be found in such publications as *Red Savina Review*, *Cream City Review*, *Reunion: The Dallas Review* and *Whale Road Review*, among others. She lives in New Jersey with her happy little family and her faithful dog Comet, who flies through the air with the greatest of ease. You can learn more about her at www.sarahghoshal.com or find her on Twitter, @sarahghoshal.

Sherine Elise Gilmour graduated with an M.F.A. in Poetry from New York University. She was recently nominated for a Pushcart Prize, and her poems have appeared or are forthcoming from *American Journal of Poetry*, *Green Mountains Review*, Oxford University Press, *Public Pool*, *River Styx*, *So To Speak*, *Tinderbox*, and other publications.

Sonia Greenfield's work has appeared in a variety of journals and anthologies. Her first book, *Boy with a Halo at the Farmer's Market*, was the winner of the 2014 Codhill Poetry Prize. She lives with her husband and son in Los Angeles where she co-directs the Southern California Poetry Festival and edits the *Rise Up Review*. More at soniagreenfield.com.

Elise Gregory tends gardens, sheep, goats, chickens, three human children, and one spouse. Her poems have appeared in *Stoneboat*, *Rock & Sling*, *Sweet: A Literary Confection*, *Cider Press Review*, *Women Arts Quarterly* and elsewhere. Her second chapbook is forthcoming from dancing girl press. *All We Can Hold: Poems of Motherhood*, which she co-edited with Emily Gwinn was published by Sage Hill Press in 2016. www.allwecanhold.com

Atoosa Grey is a poet and songwriter living in Brooklyn, NY. Her chapbook, *Black Hollyhock*, was published in the fall of 2015 by Finishing Line Press. Her poems have also appeared in journals including *Mom Egg Review*, *Best American Poetry* online, *Eunoia Review*, and *Right Hand Pointing*.

Holly Guran, author of *River of Bones* and the chapbooks *River Tracks* and *Mothers' Trails*, earned a Massachusetts Cultural Council award, and is a member of Jamaica Pond Poets. Her work has appeared in journals including *Poet Lore*, *Poetry East*, *Hawai'i Pacific Review*, *Borderlands*, *Worcester Review*, and *Salamander*. Holly resides in Boston with her husband, Phil, and their dog, Ginger.

Heather Haldeman lives in Pasadena, California. She has been married to her husband, Hank, for thirty-eight years and has three grown children. Her work has been published in *The Christian Science Monitor*, *Chicken Soup for the Soul*, *From Freckles to Wrinkles*, *Grandmother Earth*, *Mom Egg Review* and numerous online journals. She has received first, second and third prizes for her essays. Currently, she is working on a two-part memoir about growing up in wealth and ruin in Los Angeles during the Mad Men era. Visit her blog at Heatherhaldeman.blogspot.com

Lisa Kagan is a multimedia artist, writer and educator. Her business, Family Heirloom Arts, is dedicated to helping families celebrate their life stories through the creation of illustrated heirloom books. Lisa is also the director of the Art of Motherhood program, which supports mothers of young children to share their stories through art and writing workshops and publication in the online Art of Motherhood Community Gallery. FamilyHeirloomArts.com

Crystal Karlberg is a graduate of the Creative Writing Program at Boston University. Her work has been published in *Oddball Magazine*; *Tupelo Quarterly*; *MadHat Lit*; *The Prompt*; and *Best New Poets 2015*.

Donna Katzin is a poet and founding executive director of Shared Interest, a social investment fund benefiting more than 2.2 million low-income Southern Africans since 1994. She is the proud mother of Daniel and Sari Altschuler, a director of the Thembani International Guarantee Fund and Center for Community Change, and author of *With These Hands* – poems for South Africa's democracy.

Jody Keisner's writing has appeared in *The Threepenny Review*, *Brevity*, *Hunger Mountain*, *Brain,Child: the magazine for thinking mothers*, *So To Speak: A feminist journal of language and art*, *Literary Mama*, *New Writing: The International Journal for the Practice and Theory of Creative Writing*, *Assay: A Journal of Nonfiction Studies*, *VIDA Review*, and elsewhere.

Tina Kelley's third poetry collection, *Abloom and Awry*, comes out this month from CavanKerry Press, joining *Precise* (Word Press), and *The Gospel of Galore*, winner of a 2003 Washington State Book Award. She co-authored *Almost Home: Helping Kids Move from Homelessness to Hope*, and reported for *The New York Times* for ten years, sharing in a Pulitzer for 9/11 coverage. https://tinakelleypoetry.wordpress.com/

Since cataloging her book collection in third grade, **Sarah Key** has been smitten with storytelling. She has authored eight cookbooks, essays for the Huffington Post, poems in journals such as *Poet Lore, Minerva Rising, Tuesday; An Art Project*, and inclusion in two anthologies. She is grateful for her students in the Bronx who teach her how words become a lifeline.

Athena Kildegaard is the author of four books of poetry, most recently *Ventriloquy* (Tinderbox Editions). She teaches at the University of Minnesota, Morris. https://athenakildegaard.com/

Dr. Juanita Kirton earned MFA from Goddard College. She is a member of Women Who Write, Inc., and participates in Women Reading Aloud workshop series. She directs QuillEssence Writing Collective and Blairstown Writers Group. Juanita is published in several anthologies and is currently on the editorial staff for *Clock House Literary Magazine*. Juanita resides in Northeast PA, with her spouse and is a US Army Veteran.

Elizabeth Knapp (http://elizabeth-knapp.com/) is the author of *The Spite House*, winner of the 2010 De Novo Poetry Prize. The recipient of awards from *Literal Latté* and *Iron Horse Literary Review*, she has published poems in *Best New Poets 2007, The Massachusetts Review, Mid-American Review*, and *Spoon River Poetry Review*, among others. She teaches at Hood College in Frederick, Maryland.

Pamela L. Laskin is a lecturer in the English Department at City College, where she directs the Poetry Outreach Center. Several of her children's and poetry books have been published, and *Ronit And Jamil, A Palestinian/Israeli Romeo And Juliet* in verse will be published by Harper Collins in 2017. Follow her: twitter@RonitandJamil and follow her blog: http://PamelaLaskin.blogspot.com/

Kristin Laurel is a mother of three whose latest project has been exploring the layers of grief and recovery due to the sudden loss of her sister's two children. Her work can be seen in *CALYX, Gravel, r.kv.r.y* and numerous others. Her first book, *Giving Them All Away*, won the Sinclair Poetry prize from Evening Street Press.

Joan Leotta has been playing with words on page and stage since childhood. Her first poetry chapbook, *Languid Lusciousness with Lemon*, will be out in March 2017 from Finishing Line. Her daughter is still a source of inspiration. You can find her on the beach or online at www.joanleotta.wordpress.com and Joan Leotta, Author and Story Performer on Facebook (https://www.facebook.com/Joan-Leotta-Author-and-Story-Performer-188479350973/).

Issa Lewis is a graduate of New England College's MFA in Poetry program and currently teaches composition at Davenport University. She was the 2013 recipient of the Lucille Clifton Poetry Prize, and her poems have previously appeared in *Tule Review, Jabberwock, Blue Lyra Review, Pearl*, and *Naugatuck River Review*.

Judith Lichtendorf - I spent most of my professional life as an advertising copywriter. I'm old-ish, widowed, with one son, one daughter-in-law and four step-daughters. Plus two grandchildren, who are perfect. Since retiring, I have been trying to write memoir and fiction. It's both hard and fun.

Tsaurah Litzky writes poetry, fiction, prose, erotica, memoir, plays and commentary. Her poetry collections are *Baby On The Water* (Long Shot Press) and *Cleaning The Duck* (Bowery Books). Her seventeenth poetry chapbook, *Full Lotus*, (Nightballet Press) was published in October 2016. She is a collage artist and Yoga teacher. Tsaurah believes it's a privilege to be a poet.

Mary Makofske's book *Traction* (Ashland, 2011) won the Richard Snyder Award. Her other books are *The Disappearance of Gargoyles* and *Eating Nasturtiums,* winner of a Flume Press chapbook competition. Her poems have appeared recently in *Poetry East, Southern Poetry Review, Slant, Antiphon*, and *Earth's Daughters*. A new book is forthcoming from Aldrich Press in 2017.

Jessica Martinez grew up and lived in several European countries before relocating to Greater Hartford, Connecticut with her young family. Her latest poems appeared in *Literary Mama, Mom Egg Review* Vol. 14 and *Lead me to the Waters* - Selected Texts from the Daniil Pashkoff Prize 2016.

Cathy McArthur (aka, Cathy Palermo) recently published poetry in *Juked, The Cider Press Review* and in *Blueline*. Her work has also appeared in *Barrow Street, Hanging Loose, Lumina, The Valparaiso Poetry Review*, and *The Bellevue Literary Review,* among others. She teaches creative writing and composition at The City College of New York.

Kathleen McCoy's first book, *Green and Burning,* was published by Word Tech in 2016, and her chapbook *More Water Than Words* will be released in April 2017 by Finishing Line Press. Her poems have been published in *Sojourner, Tupelo 30/30 Project,* and other journals. She teaches in upstate New York.

Megan Merchant is mostly forthcoming. She is the author of two full-length poetry collections: *Gravel Ghosts* (Glass Lyre Press, 2016 Book of the Year), *The Dark's Humming* (2015 Lyrebird Prize, Glass Lyre Press, forthcoming 2017), four chapbooks, and a children's book with Philomel Books. You can find her work at meganmerchant.wix.com/poet.

Elaine Mintzer has been published in journals and anthologies including *Subprimal Review*, Lucid Moose Lit's *Like a Girl* anthology, *The Ekphrastic Review, Cultural Weekly, Rattle,* and *The Lindenwood Review*. Her work was featured in *13 Los Angeles Poets*. Elaine's first collection, *Natural Selections*, was published by Bombshelter Press. She writes and teaches writing in Los Angeles.

Judith H. Montgomery's poems appear in *Prairie Schooner, Cave Wall,* and *Rattle*, among other journals, as well as in several anthologies. Her chapbook, *Passion*, received the 2000 Oregon Book Award for Poetry; *Red Jess* (Cherry Grove Collections, 2006) and *Pulse & Constellation* (Finishing Line Press, 2007) followed. "Waiting Room" appears in her new manuscript, *Litany for Wound and Bloom*.

Deena November holds an MFA in Poetry from Carlow University. In 2005, she co-edited the anthology *I Just Hope It's Lethal* for Houghton Mifflin. Her poems have also appeared in *Nerve Cowboy, Chiron Review,* and *Keyhole Magazine* among other publications. In 2012, Hyacinth Girl Press published her first chapbook titled, *Dick Wad*. She has taught at Seton Hill University and Carlow University. Currently she teaches at Robert Morris University and the Art Institute Pittsburgh. She runs the Staghorn Poetry Series readings and workshops and is currently editing *Nasty Woman & Bad Hombres* Anthology for Lascaux Editions.

Rebecca Hart Olander's poetry has appeared recently in *Brilliant Corners, Yemassee Journal,* and *Radar Poetry,* and her critical work has been published in *Rain Taxi Review of Books, Solstice Literary Magazine,* and *Valparaiso Poetry Review*. Rebecca lives in Western Massachusetts where she teaches writing at Westfield State University and is the editor and director of Perugia Press. Website: https://rebeccahartolander.com

Eve Packer Bronx-born, poet/performer/actress--3 poetry books, most recent, *new nails* (Fly By Night Press), 5 poetry/jazz CD's, 4 w/Noah Howard; 1 w/Stephanie Stone& Daniel Carter. Teaches at Westchester Community College. Mom, grandmom, lives downtown, swims daily.

Julianne Palumbo's poems, short stories, and essays have been published in numerous literary journals. She is the author of *Into Your Light* (Flutter Press, 2013) and *Announcing the Thaw* (Finishing Line Press, 2014), poetry chapbooks about raising teenagers. She is the Founder of *Mothers Always Write*, an online literary magazine about motherhood, which can be found here: http://mothersalwayswrite.com.

Theta Pavis is director of Student Media at New Jersey City University and works with first generation college students. Her poems have appeared in *The Journal of New Jersey Poets, The Red Wheelbarrow, Emotive Fruition,* and *Mom Egg Review*. She loves to travel; her last adventure was a three-day train trip across the U.S. with her daughter. www.thetapavis.com

Lara Payne lives in Maryland. She teaches writing in the Washington, D.C. and Maryland public schools and at the College level. She has two young daughters and an unkempt house. She has been a resident of the Virginia Center for the Creative Arts and a semi-finalist for the Nation/Discovery Award.

Linda Tomol Pennisi's books are *Seamless* (Perugia, 2003). *Suddenly, Fruit* (Carolina Wren, 2006) and a chapbook *Minuscule Boxes in the Bird's Bright Throat* (Toadlily, 2014). Poems have appeared in *Calyx, Cimarron Review, Mc Sweeney's Book of Poets Picking Poets, The Cortland Review* and *Hunger Mountain*. She serves as Writer-in-Residence in the creative writing program at Le Moyne College in Syracuse, NY.

Elizabeth Poreba lives in Manhattan. A mother of two and grandmother of three, she taught English in New York City high schools for 35 years and now volunteers with the Merchant's House Museum and Citizens' Climate Lobby. Her poems have appeared in Ducts.org, *Feminist Studies in Religion, New Verse News, Written River, First Literary Review East* and *Commonweal,* among others.

Zara Raab's books are *Swimming the Eel, Fracas & Asylum, The Book of Gretel,* and *Rumpelstiltskin, or What's in a Name.* "Wasn't I Whole Once" was inspired initially by Andrew Marvell's account of birth in which "the last the master-wave / Upon the rock his mother drave; / And there she split against the stone". Raab lives in western Massachusetts.

Gwen North Reiss - Pen and Brush recently published a group of Reiss's poems called "Paper Aperture" as part of their e-publication program. She studied poetry at the 92nd Street Y and was the recipient, in 2012, of the Unterberg Poetry Center's Rachel Wetzsteon Prize. She has a degree in Literature from Yale and works as a writer and communications consultant.

Catherine Rockwood's poetry has appeared in *Concīs, The Fem, Literary Imagination* and *Literary Mama,* among other places. Reviews and essays in *Rain Taxi, Strange Horizons,* and *Tin House Magazine* (forthcoming). She lives in Massachusetts with her family.

A native New Yorker, founder of the Myth/Folklore Center at IUP, **Rosaly Roffman** taught, and edited the journal *Aristeia*. She has collaborated on 23 pieces with other artists and is the author of four published books including *Going To Bed Whole, In The Fall Of A Sparrow* (commissioned by the PA Governors Institute) and *I Want To Thank My Eyes* (Tebot-Bach). Recipient of a Distinguished Faculty Award, the BBC brought her to England to tape a "Writer from Abroad" segment. She lives in Pittsburgh PA, facilitates the well-known Squirrel Hill Poetry Workshop and is a strong believer in the healing power of poetry.

Lois Roma-Deeley's fourth collection of poems, *The Short List of Certainties,* won the Jacopone da Todi Book Prize (Franciscan University Press, 2017). She is the author the following poetry collections: *High Notes* (2011, a Paterson Poetry Prize Finalist); *northSight* (2006); *Rules of Hunger* (2004). Her poems have been featured in numerous literary journals and anthologies. http://www.loisroma-deeley.com/

Margaret Rozga has published four books of poetry, including *Pestiferous Questions* (Lit Fest Press 2017). She writes a monthly op-ed for *Milwaukee Neighborhood News* and has had work appear recently in *Los Angles Art News* and the anthology *All We Can Hold.*

Sharon Scholl is professor emerita from Jacksonville University (Fl) where she taught humanities and non-western studies. Her chapbook, *Summer's Child,* is published by Finishing Line Press (2016). A professional musician, she maintains a website, freeprintmusic.com, that gives away free music for small groups.

Ada Jill Schneider is the author of *This Once-Only World, Behind the Pictures I Hang, The Museum of My Mother, Fine Lines and Other Wrinkles,* and several chapbooks. Winner of the National Galway Kinnell Poetry Prize, she has reviewed books for Midstream Magazine and directs "The Pleasure of Poetry" at the Somerset Public Library in Massachusetts. www.adajillschneider.com

Carla Schwartz's poems have appeared in *Aurorean, ArLiJo, Fourth River Review, Fulcrum, Common Ground, Cactus Heart, Switched-on Gutenberg, Poetry Quarterly, Naugatuck River Review, Solstice Magazine,* and *Ibbetson Street.* Her book, *Mother, One More Thing* is available at online retailers. Her CB99videos youtube channel has had 300,000+ views. Learn more at carlapoet.com, or her blog, wakewiththesun.blogspot.com.

Lore Segal is the author of *Shakespeare's Kitchen,* a finalist for the Pulitzer Prize, as well as the novels *Lucinella, Other People's Houses,* and *Her First American.* She is the recipient of an American Academy of Arts and Letters award, a Guggenheim Fellowship, an O. Henry Award, and the Harold U. Ribalow Prize. She has written for *The New Yorker, The New York Times Book Review, The New Republic,* and other publications. She also writes children's books and translates from the German. Segal lives and works in New York City.

Lynne Shapiro is a writer and educator. Her poems and essays have been published in such journals as *CV2, Mslexia, Terrain.org., Mom Egg Review,* and *Platte Valley Review* and in anthologies such as *Eating Her Wedding Dress, A Collection of Clothing Poems* and *Decomposition: An Anthology of Fungi Inspired Poems.* She recently co-edited *Dark As A Hazel Eye, Coffee and Chocolate Poems* for Ragged Sky Press.

Anna Sheppard is a freelance photographer serving the Treasure Coast. Capturing moments in time for all to enjoy is her daily inspiration. http://annasheppardphotography.zenfolio.com www.instagram.com/annasheppardphotography

Sally Bishop Shigley teaches literature, literary theory, and the intersection between neuroscience and literature at Weber State University in Ogden, Utah. Her essay "Great Expectations: Infertility, Disability, Possibility" is forthcoming in *The History of Infertility* (Palgrave) and her essay co-written with Lauren Fowler appears in *Rethinking Empathy through Literature* (Routledge 2014).

Ana C. H. Silva lives Olive, NY and in NYC. Her poetry has been published in *Podium, Mom Egg Review, the nth position, Snow Monkey, Anemone Sidecar, Chronogram,* and *Stepaway Magazine*. She won the inaugural Rachel Wetzsteon Memorial Poetry Prize at the 92ndSt. Y Unterberg Poetry Center.

John Warner Smith's poems have appeared in *Ploughshares, Callaloo, Antioch Review, Tupelo Quarterly, Quiddity, Transition,* and other literary journals. He is the author of full-length poetry collections *Soul Be A Witness* (MadHat Press) and *A Mandala of Hands* (Aldrich Press/Kelsay Books). Smith's poems have been nominated for a Pushcart Prize and for the Sundress *Best of the Net* Anthology. A Cave Canem Fellow, Smith earned his MFA in Creative Writing at the University of New Orleans. He teaches English at Southern University in Baton Rouge and runs a non-profit organization dedicated to education reform in Louisiana. Smith's poetry can be found at www.johnwarnersmith.com.

Deborah L. Staunton's work has appeared in *The Sondheim Review, Writers' Journal, Sheepshead Review, Mothers Always Write, Meat For Tea, The MacGuffin and Chicken Soup for the Soul.*. She has written child development materials for Harcourt Learning Direct and is currently working on her memoir, *Between Love & Madness*.

Autumn Stephens is the author of the *Wild Women* series of women's history and humor, editor of two personal essay anthologies, and former co-editor of *The East Bay Monthly*. She has written for *The New York Times,* the *San Francisco Chronicle,* and numerous other publications. She conducts writing workshops for cancer survivors in Oakland, Calif., and teaches private writing classes.

Alison Stone is the author of five collections, including *Ordinary Magic, Dangerous Enough,* and *They Sing at Midnight,* which won the 2003 Many Mountains Moving Award. Her poems have appeared in The Paris Review, Poetry, Ploughshares, and many others. She was awarded *Poetry*'s Frederick Bock Prize and *New York Quarterly*'s Madeline Sadin award. She is a licensed psychotherapist.

Laura-Gray Street is author of *Pigment* and *Fume* (Salmon Poetry) and *Shift Work* (forthcoming from Red Bird Chapbooks), and co-editor with Ann Fisher-Wirth of *The Ecopoetry Anthology* (Trinity UP). She is associate professor of English and directs the Creative Writing Program at Randolph College in Lynchburg, VA. More at www.lauragraystreet.com.

Judy Swann is a poet, essayist, translator, mom, blogger, and bicycle commuter, whose work has been published in many venues both in print and online, including the *Mom Egg Review*. Her son is (always) on his way home. Her book, *We Are All Well: The Letters of Nora Hall* has given her great joy. She loves. She lives in Ithaca, NY.

Although she is a native French speaker, **Ariane Synovitz** enjoys writing in English. She writes short stories, postcard prose and poetry, some of which has been published in English-language online magazines. She has written creative non-fiction in French for her own program "Les Mots d'Ariane" on Radio France Prague. She lives in Prague, Czech Republic, with her husband and son.

Mariahadessa Ekere Tallie is the author of *Karma's Footsteps* and *Dear Continuum: Letters to a Poet Crafting Liberation* and a mother of three otherwordly daughters. Her work is the subject of the film *I Leave My Colors Everywhere*. www.ekretallie.com

Jane Vincent Taylor is a poet, teacher, and creative collaborator. Her book of narrative poems, *The Lady Victory*, was adapted for the stage at Michigan State University. Her latest book, *Pencil Light*, was the source of an exhibition of pencil drawings at Artspace at Untitled Gallery. Jane teaches creative writing at Ghost Ranch in Abiquiu, New Mexico and lives in Oklahoma City.

Claudia Van Gerven is a retired writing instructor at the University of Colorado, Boulder. Her poems have been published in a number national and international journals and anthologies. She has won a number of national awards. She has four chapbooks published, *The Ends of Sunbonnet Sue,* which won the 1997 Angel Fish Press Prize, *Amazing Grace* (Green Fuse, 2010), *Bearing Witness* (Finishing Line 2014), and *Totem* (Green Fuse, 2014)**.**

Susan Vespoli lives in downtown Phoenix and is the mother of three grown kids. She received her MFA from Antioch University L.A., has a chapbook called *Road Trip* published by *Dancing Girl Press*, plus poetry and prose published online/in print at spots such as *Mom Egg Review, New Verse News, Verse Wisconsin*, and *Writing Bloody.*

Faith Williams lives in DC with husband and two dogs, and before retirement was a children's librarian in a number of DC schools and libraries, and for years before that taught English. She has published poems in *Mom Egg Review, Poet Lore, Nimrod International, Sow's Ear, Kansas Quarterly, Tinderbox, Xanadu,* and *Comstock Review*, among others.

Dara Herman Zierlein is a political artist, art educator and mother, a passionate artist focusing on women's rights, motherhood, equal rights and climate change. Dara is the founder of Supermom Unveiled, a resource website for women and men around the paradigm of parenthood. Dara is the author of "Don't Eat The Plastic", her first children's book. Blog: https://motherstime.blogspot.com/ Review: http://www.supermomunveiled.com/our_mission

MOM EGG REVIEW

Mom Egg Review Back Issues Available

Vol. 14 "Change"	2016	Paper, 128 pp. $18
Vol. 13 "Compassionate Action"	2015	Paper, 154 pp. $18
Vol. 12	2014	Paper, 150 pp. $18
Vol. 11 "Mother Tongue"	2013	Paper, 125 pp. $18
Vol. 10 "The Body"	2012	Paper, 120 pp. $18
Vol. 9	2011	Paper, 120 pp. $18
Vol. 8 "Lessons"	2010	Paper, 120 pp. $18
Vol. 7	2009	Paper, 124 pp. $18

*Plus US shipping $3.50 for the first book, $1.00 for each additional book.

Email info@themomegg.com for info about discounts for quantity purchases and for classroom use, or for out-of-country shipping.

Subscribe to *MER*

US shipping is free for subscription copies!

One year $18
Two years $36

Mail your order with a check to

Mom Egg Review
Half-Shell Press
PO Box 9037
Bardonia, NY 10954

Contact: info@themomegg.com

Order on the web at
www.momeggreview.com (Click "Shop")

MOM EGG REVIEW
Literature & Art

Made in the USA
San Bernardino, CA
19 March 2017